To Sea with "Sanu"

To Sea with "Sanu"

DENYS VAL BAKER

illustrated by

DONALD SWAN

JOHN BAKER
5 Royal Opera Arcade, Pall Mall,
London, S.W.1

©
1967
DENYS VAL BAKER
First published 1967 by
John Baker (Publishers) Ltd
5 Royal Opera Arcade, Pall Mall,
London
S.W.1

FOR FRANK AND KATE BAKER
IN MEMORY OF MANY
HAPPY CRUISES

Printed in Great Britain by
Billing & Sons Limited at Guildford

Contents

Author's Note

In some previous autobiographical books, *The Sea's in the Kitchen*, *The Door is Always Open* and *We'll Go Round the World Tomorrow*, I portrayed the life of a writer with a large family in a house at the edge of the sea in St. Ives, Cornwall. As the title of the last volume suggests, we have recently become more personally involved with the hazards and delights of life *at* sea, following the acquisition of an elderly motor fishing vessel. *To Sea with "Sanu"* tells the whole story of what has proved to be an exciting and often very amusing adventure — from the wistful dream to the formidable reality, from those early nervous coastal "hops" to much more strenuous voyages to Paris and the Western Isles of Scotland (not forgetting a traumatic "quiet week-end on the Scillies"). In a sense, then, *To Sea with "Sanu"* continues the autobiographical saga: but in another sense I have tried to make it a book on its own, a simple, fairly practical account of one family's introduction to the incredible pleasures of cruising around in a boat of your own. My simple advice to anyone who might feel encouraged, after reading the book, to consider following our example is — yes, *do*. You will never regret such a step; and in fact, whole new vistas will be opened up in your life. Good luck!

1

The Dream of Fair Women

WHERE some men dream about fair women my own dreams, for many years, have focused upon boats. Like women boats are thought about in physical terms : one contemplates with sensual pleasure a boat's lines, the grace with which it moves through the water, the flutter of a pretty sail in the wind. But in fact the attraction of a boat lies far beyond merely what it is or how it looks. The really exciting thing about a boat is that it offers a whole new kind of freedom, a way of life – travel, adventure, strange places, new faces, islands in the sun. Little wonder that as far back as I can remember I used to lean over harbour walls staring down upon the array of colourful boats with hungry, envious eyes. One day . . .!

Looking back I can see that this strange love affair with boats has been with me all the time. As a child I lived at Hampton Court on the River Thames, and often in the summer evenings I used to walk along the towpaths staring with avid interest at the clusters of moored boats of all shapes and sizes. I was naturally intrigued by some of the bizarre and enormous houseboats, moored along Tagg's Island like strange white castles, sometimes rising to three floor-levels. They seldom seemed to be occupied during the week but on weekends the tarpaulins would be thrown back, windows open wide, and to the sound of tinny gramophone music exotic-looking individuals (some even wearing yachting caps) could be seen wandering about. I would envy these people bitterly even though my parents pointed out sensibly that they might as well be living on dry land for all the travelling their boats did. On the

A*

other hand this was not altogether true. I have never forgotten looking up one evening when shadows were beginning to fall and seeing the astonishing apparition of a ghostly white houseboat gliding silently down the middle of the river. It was in fact being towed by a motor boat from one mooring site to another – but the effect remained memorable.

Houseboats were, of course, only one kind of craft. I could also feast my youthful eyes on long chromium plated cruisers, bright gleaming yachts, long open motor cruisers, and many other vessels – including, miracle of miracles, an occasional ocean-going schooner with tall masts and the air of having just returned from Tahiti. One of these I have always remembered. She must have been nearly seventy feet long, and perhaps as many years old – a sleek white yacht with everything spotlessly clean and polished brass rails. The decks were of teak, and so were the cabin tops – the whole boat glistened and gleamed and echoed romance. She lay at her mooring with a strange, lissome air, as if utterly bored and dissatisfied with shore life, and waiting only to be sailed away. It was not very difficult for a romantic boy to imagine those great white sails unfurled and booming out, and the sharp prow cutting through the water as the skilful helmsman (me) turned her round and headed down river.

I never saw that yacht sail away, but my longing to be associated with boats continued to grow. Soon with a friend I began hiring out the rather old-fashioned skiffs which can still be seen lined up along the banks at boathouses in the Hampton Court area. My friend was used to rowing and he managed to instil in me the necessity for turning the oar and feathering, so that after a while we managed to get along at quite a fair pace. Later we changed to punts, those strange flat-bottomed craft that are for ever associated in one's mind with Jerome K. Jerome's *Three Men in a Boat*. How satisfying it was to glide down with the tide, occasionally giving a gentle pull with the paddles . . . everywhere there was absolute stillness except for the ripples made by the punt. . . .

Oh, yes, the river could be a magical and marvellous place.

Soon after this my friend acquired what was known as a Rob Roy canoe, a Canadian type, very long and very strong, the old-fashioned canoe such as one remembers seeing Red Indians using in the old films. It had a high turned-up prow, and the same kind of stern, and altogether made a striking impression. We felt very superior when, after loading our camping equipment and provisions, we set off up the River Thames for a week's canoeing holiday. It was exciting, too, for with a canoe one can explore every nook and cranny en route, which is just what we did. Once or twice we encountered alarums, such as being carried unexpectedly towards a weir when we were meant to head for a lock, but in general our journey was a smooth one. I was exhilarated by my first taste of travelling on water, and hankered for wider experiences.

For some years such experiences remained fleeting ones. As a boy scout I made a memorable trip to France by cross-channel steamer; calm as a river going out – so rough coming back that we were all miserably sick. Later, whenever possible I would sneak similar trips. Holidaying in North Wales I would make a bee line for Llandudno in order to travel on the steamer that called in there en route for Menai Bridge; staying for a while in pre-Beatle Liverpool. I was for ever catching the ferry-boats to New Brighton and Wallasey and back again; finding myself in Weston super Mare and coming across a magic poster advertisement, I rushed to board the pleasure steamer going across to Penarth and Cardiff. Mundane such trips may seem to the hardened sea traveller, but to me they were touched with gold. I shall never forget another occasion, during a holiday in Cornwall, when my parents took me on the ferry-boat from Falmouth to St. Mawes and we crossed that wonderful wide estuary thronged with maritime traffic. Was it some premonition, I wonder, that made me feel so strangely exhilarated – as if on the threshold of all kinds of wonderful experiences?

In fact, life went on in a fairly humdrum way. I went to live at
Tring, Hertfordshire, not far from the Grand Union Canal, and
inevitably wandered along the grassy banks. Often I would come
across a convoy of commercial barges chugging by, bright and
colourful with their painted bows and sterns, and manned by
engaging gipsy-like families whose lives, somehow, I would find
myself envying. It may well have been then that I began to take
more interest in the possibilities of boats not merely as a means of
an hour or two's pleasure on the river, but as representing a way of
life. I envied the children of those canal families, living on their
boats, travelling from one place to another – how could their lives
ever be dull or ordinary like mine? Something about those barges
certainly stuck in my mind and many years later, when I began
looking seriously for a boat, I was always drawn to the large
beamy boats such as the Dutch Jonkers or the old Thames barges.

For many more years I followed the life of a free-lance author,
marrying and accumulating several small children, and all this
time, with curious perversity, lived by the sea, yet never embarked
upon it. This was in Cornwall, a strange and haunted place where
life is permanently dominated by the sea. Living at Sennen Cove,
just by Land's End, I would spend hours walking along the beach
and watching the huge waves pounding across Whitsand Bay . . .
or climb out on the rocks of Cape Cornwall, where spray and froth
would be hurled higher than the house tops. Occasionally, looking
out to sea, I would spy some tramp steamer battling its way round
the Longship Lighthouse and marvel at such venturesome spirits.
But I do not think I had any premonition that the day would
come when I, too, might become that speck on the horizon.

And yet it was now, constantly by the sound of breakers booming on rocks and sand, and in my late thirties, that I began to take
a much more active interest in boating. In typical Scorpio fashion,
living by the sea, I chose instead the more devious method of
taking my family on a river cruise. I had often seen the advertisements for boats to be hired for cruises, and finally took the plunge

and rented a motor cruiser for a fortnight's trip up the River Thames. This was the first time in my life I had ever handled a motor-boat, and though ours was a simple enough 35-footer with diesel engine and quite luxurious accommodation, I managed to commit the usual gaffs, like ramming a lock gate and running aground. Despite this we meandered our way via Runnymede, Maidenhead, Marlow and Henley and back again without, rather to my surprise, any major disaster.

After this, our annual family cruise became almost a routine of life. The following year I took the family up to Norfolk where we spent a lively fortnight on the Broads, experiencing the sometimes disturbing problems of a tidal river and also the even more alarming aspects of handling a sailing dinghy. The year afterwards I decided to try a canal holiday. We hired a boat from Chester and chugged our way, via about fifty locks, down the Shropshire Union Canal and then up the winding lovely Llangollen Canal, and over Telford's famous Pontcysylltau acqueduct which crosses 120 feet above the River Dee. Finally we embarked on our most ambitious project of all, the whole family flying across to Dublin and then proceeding to Roosky for a lengthy exploration of the River Shannon. This was a new and challenging experience, for not only was the river very wide, it gradually spanned out into a series of large lakes, one of them measuring twenty-six miles long and three miles wide. Not without good reason the guide book warned me that in these lakes a change of weather "can result in creating a short steep sea far worse than anything to be encountered in coastal waters". In fact I often think this Shannon experience marked the water-shed in the devious relationship between myself and boats and water, for on this occasion we were covering such large areas of river that in fact it was necessary to give really serious study to the problems of navigation and buoyage. Parts of Lough Derg were so wide that in poor visibility it was not possible to see the next buoy and one was, so to speak, lost at sea. It was very much a testing time, and owing to the fact that we went early in April and encountered much blustery weather and "short steep seas", I found I had to apply what seamanship I had picked up, and improvise a good deal more. Previously I would never have imagined myself capable of such a feat . . . and so, all at once, I began to acquire a new, perhaps rash, but steadily growing confidence.

Back in Cornwall my wife Jess and I began attending navigation classes at Penzance. Some years before, in London, we had attended similar classes at a local technical school, but in those days it was something of a dilettante experiment. We caught a bus down to a school in Lambeth and sat in a dinghy classroom just off the Elephant and Castle dutifully plotting imaginary sea courses off Land's End or the Lizard, and it all seemed sadly unreal. Now, somehow, it was not unreal. How could it be when we came out from the class and gazed over Mount's Bay towards the Lizard itself? Or when Land's End lay only ten miles to the west? There was a further point too: in London many of the students had been dreamers like ourselves — here were were surrounded mostly by young fishermen who were actually going to sea and there was such a business-like air about everything that one felt really committed.

Every Thursday Jess and I made the ten-mile journey from St. Ives to Penzance where the classes were held at the same grammar school as our son Stephen attended by day. It was a strange experience being back in a class-room and sitting at worn desks inscribed with names of dozens of past occupants. Our instructor was Captain Harvey of Sennen, a retired master who in his time had been all over the world. He delighted in illustrating his lessons with dry stories of navigators who had made "very slight" mistakes — like taking the wrong side of a buoy and running a 700-ton tanker upon to a sandy beach. Captain Harvey's method of teaching was simple and direct. Each lesson he would introduce us to one main new facet of navigation, like taking a fix, or estimating a course, and focus upon that until it was really fixed in our minds.

At the beginning of the next course he would go over the previous lesson once more, so that we remembered it all, and then pass on to yet another facet. I think most of us felt we had managed to take in the information, but when towards the end of the lesson we were set some practical examples – then the fun began, and worried frowns began to crease our faces! Mathematics have never been my strong point and I would find it hard going, but Jess, who did a chemistry degree, was quick off the mark usually. All the same there were times when we would both sit back feeling absolutely baffled, having plotted a course that landed us several miles inland instead of at sea!

"Don't worry," said Captain Harvey kindly. "You'll find that with more practical experience you'll really absorb these lessons."

So we kept manfully attending, even when often it was the last thing we felt like doing. Later we were indeed to be very glad of the efforts, for though we did not by any means finish off a complete course of navigation, we did absorb quite a useful smattering of information. About buoys, for instance – for coastal work it is imperative to have a simple understanding of the main kinds of buoyage. Put simply: red and white buoys are fixed on the port side entering an estuary, black and white buoys mark the starboard side, and the navigator sees to it that his ship passes between them, whether going up or down. Put another way, he keeps to the right-hand side of any port buoy, and to the left-hand side of any starboard buoy.

We were also given a grounding in taking fixes on landmarks, or other ships, or lights; we studied tidal streams and their effects; and we learned how to read tide levels. Above all, we became familiar with charts and their various markings, and how to recognise the information printed thereon. By the time we ended our lessons we knew how to bring a boat in and out of port and how to take it from point A to point B – at least on paper!

And so, almost without realising, I found I had moved much closer to the sea, and that dreams of fair boats were indeed permissible. The curious thing is that from the beginning my dreams were along very definite and, I like to think, quite sensible lines. I was never a yachting type, never very much fancied racing about uncomfortably in small dinghies. I was drawn to boating for all the tangible new opportunities it offered of travel and adventure. From my point of view this meant family boating, which meant in turn that the sort of boat I was interested in would need to be a large one, big enough to live upon for long periods if necessary. At the same time, just as I have never liked modern cars and derived a great deal of pleasure out of driving old vintage cars, so I knew in my heart that I would never find much satisfaction or pleasure in the conventional modern motor cruisers with all their gaudy chrome linings and spotless white sides. No, what I fancied – well, what I fancied lay all around me, actually, at the busy fishing port of Newlyn, where often Jess and I would take a walk out along the quay. For here lined up in rows were the West Country M.F.V.s (Motor Fishing Vessels) whose shapes were already familiar to us from having lived so long in the district – boats that were sturdy and strong, roomy and beamy, whose very appearance inspired a sense of real confidence.

At this time we had considerable difficulty in maintaining ourselves and our children, let alone find money for any small extras, so to be thinking about boats in this wistful fashion—especially large motor fishing vessels – was bizarre in the extreme. Nevertheless, for the next year or so this was the irrational way in which my mind moved. I began subscribing to some of the national boating magazines, reading avidly the fascinating articles about the latest new boats, and scanning with a kind of morbid curiosity the columns of advertisements of second-hand boats. I took books out of the library about voyages round the world, devouring such gripping stories as Ann Davidson's *Last Voyage,* and Eric Hiscock's *Wanderer III* and Edward Alcard's autobiography, not forgetting some of the older classics, like Slocum's memoirs. While my normal life apparently went along in its normal way, secretly I was often elsewhere battling with the mainsail or hanging for dear life on to the wheel in a Force 8 wind out in the Atlantic. My wife, being an essentially practical person, was inclined not to waste time on the impossible, but I have never been confined by the practical or the possible, and so I was inclined to indulge on my own in these constant day-dreams. Once, many years before, I had experienced a similar feeling about Cornwall, which constantly drew me like some mysterious magnet — and here we were now living and settled in Cornwall. If that particular dream had come true, who knew but this new one, if it burned bright enough, might find similar fulfilment?

One day, while in this mood, I took a walk round the Island of St. Ives, coming across Porthgwidden and then round to the harbour quay. Suddenly I stopped in surprise, for among the cluster of fishing boats and dinghies there lay a newcomer — a large, graceful, white motor fishing vessel, very like the Newlyn boats, but obviously, on closer inspection, converted to a cruising boat. I walked slowly along the quay, trying not to appear too inquisitive. She was a lovely Scottish-type of boat, with the high prow sweeping down to the squat middle and canoe stern. Irony of ironies, this was the *Batuba*, a boat which later on I was actually to be offered; but I knew nothing of these later events, then. I only knew, as I looked down and saw all the signs of family life aboard, that here was the sort of boat I could really dream about — here was what, in the back of my mind, I was groping for. A boat which was strong enough and tough enough to take me anywhere, and which yet had a real character and attraction of its own. Henceforth, as I dreamed about my dream-boat, if I did not know that my dream would ever come true, at least the details were much clearer.

2

In Search of "Sanu"

THE first thing my wife and I did when an unexpected inheritance offered us the almost unbelievable chance to turn our dreams into reality was—to go to the Boat Show. In retrospect I was never quite sure whether to regard this as a disastrous waste of time or invaluable experience. For one hitherto safely protected from the hard facts of realising a dream the seemingly endless hours spent under the vast booming roof of Earls Court, on a cold January day, were not only exhausting, but positively confusing. Before going to the Show I had very clearly fixed in my mind exactly the sort of boat I wanted . . . no sooner had I visited a few stands, and my decisiveness began to waver. That was a very smart little ketch, wasn't it? How about this nice beamy motor cruiser? Or that new cutter? Or the Bermuda sloop? Or the fibreglass motor yacht? Or this schooner or that yawl? Or then again, what about . . .? After a couple of hours of being seduced into one boat after another, and each time beginning to think that perhaps this was really quite a suitable choice, my head began to whirl. As if that was not bad enough, after lunch we found ourselves beginning to inspect the section of do-it-yourself kits, and the monstrous delusion threatened to be born that maybe we would build our own boat!

Fortunately, at least so far as that aspect was concerned, our attention was recaptured, not by a boat at the show, but by a stand of the East Coast Yachting Agency containing a large selection of photographs and sales literature concerning a new boat they were marketing, designed by Francis Jones and now offered under the rather attractive name of the Inchcape. I read, excitedly, the explanation that these were in fact Motor Fishing Vessels, very sturdily built in Scotland on the lines of the traditional seine-net M.F.V.s which operate in all weathers off the coast of Scotland, with modifications carried out to suit yachtsmen. All Inchcapes were ketch-rigged with a useful area of canvas for steadying or off-the-wind sailing, and of course they were fitted with large and powerful modern diesel engines. Well, the sales literature was compelling enough, but when I looked at the large sepia photographs of Inchcapes on trial runs – then, indeed, the fat was in the fire. Here was just the sort of boat I had dreamed about.

Of course, at this stage I should have said: "How much?" But in fact I was caught up by such a wave of excitement that when I was told by the salesman that though the Inchcape's were too big to be shown at Earls Court there *was* a demonstration model at that moment actually moored off Hammersmith Pier – my impatience would brook no delay. I grabbed Jess by the hand and ran off to get a taxi to take us to Hammersmith as fast as possible.

When we got to the Pier, we were certainly not disappointed. There, riding quietly at the mooring, was an Inchcape 52-footer, a most graceful and attractive craft, with gleaming new fittings, shining tall masts, and a snug looking wheelhouse into which we now stepped.

Once inside I was even more impressed – everything had been laid out with sense and foresight; there was a large roomy L-shaped saloon with a modern sink unit and galley, and comfortable, indeed quite luxurious, cabins, as well as a multitude of useful navigational equipment. True the engine room seemed only big enough for a dwarf, but I was prepared to forgive this relatively small matter when the rest of the boat was such a stunner. Besides, we weren't the only prospective customers, there were two or three other couples wandering about with glazed looks like ourselves. . . . We didn't want to go on a waiting list.

Furtively I drew the salesman to one side.

"What's the earliest possible date for delivery?"

"Well, sir, let me see — how about the beginning of May?"

May? That was five months away. Still, I suppose somehow I could manage to wait. I looked at my wife for confirmation. To my surprise she was making one of those secret signals that married couples develop.

"I'll just talk it over with my wife."

"Of course, sir, make yourselves comfortable."

Alas, we did not need to settle down. My wife explained to me briskly and curtly that she had just seen the cost sheets of an Inchcape 52, and the total figure amounted to more than ten thousand pounds.

"Ten thousand?" I stuttered. "Ten Thousand?"

"Exactly. And just how much have you in the bank?"

Truth to tell, a good deal less than half of that amount. Crestfallen I avoided catching the salesman's eye and crept away, tail between legs. It was a disastrous end to a day that had opened full of excitement and promise. In fact, it was weeks before I fully got over my shock of the Inchcape, which I would have loved to have bought, for alone among new and modern boats she catered for what I was looking.

After this saddening experience I retired for a while to lick my wounds, and then returned refreshed to the fray. At least my wife was with me on the main point — a boat we had dreamed of and a boat we were now going to buy. But just how, where, or why remained to be seen. For some time, foolishly as I came to realise, I wrote round to various boat makers and boat yards inquiring about new boats. After a while it dawned on me that any new boat of my requirements was going to cost as much as an Inchcape, without being half as attractive. No, there would have to be a different approach — or rather the same approach as with motor cars: the second-hand market.

Looking back I often wonder why I didn't make use of the services of a trained surveyor, but the fact is that just as in writing I have shied from the middle-man, the literary agent, so with boats I could not bring myself to give up the gamble of searching for and finding our own boat.

"You'd better get the yachting magazines," said a friend, "plenty of boats for sale there."

This was something of an understatement. One evening I brought home a batch of the magazines and we settled down to study the ads. Hours later, dazed and exhausted, we dragged ourselves to bed, our heads reeling from the masses of close-typed information in the 'For Sale' columns.

"Cornish lugger, forty feet by twelve feet by three and a half feet, paraffin starting engine, ideal for conversion . . . auxiliary gaff cutter, eight tons, good head room, new keel bolts . . . two and a half ton blackwater sloop, all-teak decks . . . twin-screw motor cruiser, double diagonal mahogany hull, echo sounder, siren, patent log . . ." There was literally no end to the lists – in one magazine alone I counted no fewer than 645 boats for sale, quite apart from the new craft also offered.

Sometimes, it seemed to us, on that and subsequent perusals of the yachting magazines, that the world consisted of almost nothing but boats for sale. This conception was curiously reinforced in later weeks when we would travel somewhere to view a particular boat – only to find, in the same yacht basin or along the same stretch of mooring, a parade of sixty or seventy other forlorn-looking boats, all empty, all having the rather pathetic air about them, as if to say, "Please buy me – I need a good home."

If we had stopped to think about it, the factor might have seemed rather alarming. However, ours not to reason why, our job to find a boat, if possible. We began underlining the most interesting advertisements and writing off for particulars. Back came the answers, shoals and shoals of them – and, very often, photographs. Dozens and dozens of photographs of glamorous, exotic looking boats.

I don't think there was a single photograph that did not depict an attractive, thoroughly seaworthy boat. It was only when, seduced, we arranged an assignment that we found the fulfilment strangely different from anticipation.

At first I was frankly overwhelmed by the avalanche of information, but Jess, a much more practical person, bought a large file and we began assembling "our" boats in some sort of order, grading them according to price, size and geographical location. Even at that early stage it was obvious that personal inspection was essential, even though many of the boats seemed to be lying at the Channel Islands or the Outer Hebrides or some other far-flung corner of the dwindling British Empire. The simple solution seemed to be to work out a single itinerary which would enable us to inspect a maximum number of boats, and when this was done I arranged to take a week's holiday.

Our first port of call was a West Country port to which we had been attracted by glowing details of a "Trading schooner" no less than seventy-five feet in length, three-masted, and selling at a mere nine hundred pounds. We clung to all kinds of romantic conceptions until we were confronted with a sad, rotting hulk, permanently embedded into mud. "You could lift her out alright with the right equipment," said the owner, with that incredible chirpiness which all selling owners have to develop – but, wisely, we went on with our journey.

Our next visit was more cheering, this time to the smart modern office of one of the new business-executive type of ships brokers. Here a suave young man in striped trousers extracted sheaves of important looking documents from the files and bore us off in a bright new car to inspect about four enormous millionaire-type yachts. Lying near one of these monstrosities, however, was a rather nice old converted fishing boat which surprisingly, was also on our super-salesman's books. Alas, it transpired she was also on almost every other broker's books and after some quick investigation we were informed the boat was unfortunately "under offer".

With further experience we became familiar with this phrase which meant, simply, as courtship, that the object of our desire was promised to another. Naturally enough almost every boat we fancied seemed to fall into this category – real bargains were eagerly recognised and seized upon even by comparative novices like ourselves.

Indeed, as we progressed from one inspection to another – perhaps I should say, up one creek after another – we really did learn quite a bit about boats. We had of course avidly read up the books designed to protect intending boat buyers. We had a sharp eye for leaking decks, rotting ropes, rusted plates and so forth, and we knew that the advocated procedure on arrival was to produce a pen-knife and dig it into the bottom of the ship's hull (though to tell the truth we lacked the courage to commit such an act of aggression in front of the owners). What we did now learn was to rely with increasing confidence upon our own instincts. Say what you like, confidence was inspired by a clean, well looked after boat, sails neatly tied up, engine glistening and gleaming and well oiled, every spar in its proper place. On the other hand, with one boat which, on paper, had seemed to us ideal – when we finally boarded her, it was to find disconnected pipes everywhere, the engine hidden by clouds of rust, mattresses wet from rain seeping through the deck – and, final ignominy, when we wanted to get off it turned out that the owner had forgotten to replace a plug in the dinghy which now lay submerged! Such a background was not conducive to a sale.

Similarly, our imagination was caught by an advertisement of a sloop going at a very reasonable figure. The boat had just been sailed back from the Greek Islands, and altogether it sounded so good that we were suspicious as to why it was being sold. When we finally called the owner, an extrovert and loquacious gentleman in a peaked cap, explained that the sole reason was he had bought a larger boat still. He than rambled off into amusing anecdotes about his own searches for boats, how he had travelled all the way to Spain once to inspect one craft and when he put his hand out to feel the state of the bulwarks – his fingers went right through the wood, it was so rotten.

Unfortunately, while he expostulated in this fashion, my wife, a highly suspicious creature, was prodding about on the deck above and finding several very large patches of obvious dry rot.

So it went on, our search for the magic grail. We saw Bermudan sloops, auxiliary yawls, pilot cutters, motor sailers, Brixham trawlers, motor fishing vessels, admiralty pinnaces, ex-German E-boats, converted lifeboats, catamarans. . . . We visited half the boatyards on the South Coast of England, plus a few more up the East Coast, and a final sortie along the banks of the River Thames. Surprisingly enough it was at a Thames mooring that we came upon the real boat of our dreams—quite out of our price range, alas. She was a good sixty feet long with a mast almost as high, and she rode at anchor like a proud queen, flags fluttering, paint-work smart, railings agleam. She was built of teak throughout, copper-sheathed, beautifully fitted out, ready to sail down the river and out to sea at a moment's notice. And why was she like that? Because – we might have guessed – she was one of a large number of boats we came upon which, aggravatingly, were really *non*-boats.

They all belonged to wealthy men who led high pressures lives in the City of London and were always too busy to spare the time to go sailing, but liked the idea of owning a boat. I am not in any way exaggerating: on another occasion we visited a handsome motor yacht on the River Hamble, after an interview at his London business office with the owner. The boat, of course, when we saw her, was in spotless condition. We were met at the quayside by a local seaman who was actually employed full-time at a wage of ten pounds a week solely to look after the yacht. Almost the first thing this man said to us, rather peevishly, was, "Oh, hasn't Mr. X come down? Pity, I wanted a word with him. Fact is, I haven't actually seen him here for nigh on two years." This was indeed true – this particular owner had last set foot on the decks of his own boat two years before! And the amazing thing is that there are dozens more like him.

Needless to say all this questing took time, not merely weeks but several months. Looking back, this is rather exasperating for the fact is had we but known it, we found our perfect boat almost at the beginning of our search. It happened like this. One of the first boats that attracted us was moored at Lymington, Hants. We motored up and spent a pleasant evening talking with the owner, a rugged Scottish engineer who was obviously trustworthy when he vouched for the boat's reliability. Unfortunately, when we saw her she wasn't really right for our requirements, with very limited accommodation for her size. However, while in Lymington we walked past the windows of a well-known firm of yacht brokers, Laurent Giles, and there among a list of boats for sale was a photograph of a sturdy looking M.F.V. On the off chance I went in and obtained details, and as she was lying at Moody's yard at Southampton we decided to drive over and have a look.

In this manner, one sunny autumn day, we had our first sight of the M.F.V. *Sanu*, registered tonnage 23.45 tons, other vital statistics, 60 ft. 9 in. length, by 18 ft. beam by 7½ ft. draft. . . .

At this time *Sanu* was lying on a mud berth beside another more modern M.F.V. which was also for sale. We had a look at both of them, but had some difficulty in getting aboard *Sanu*, and I had to go wandering round the shipyard trying to track down the keys. Jess meanwhile stayed aboard. When I came back I was surprised to find her still sitting at the bow of the boat, a curious far-away look on her face. She looked at me significantly and smiled.

"This is the boat for us – I KNOW."

It was so unlike my wife to make such a quick and certain decision (usually I have the hunches) that subconsciously I began to react in the opposite way.

"She's a bit big, isn't she? I mean do you think we could cope? And that engine! Must weigh tons!"

All the same as we began to look around *Sanu* I had to share much of my wife's excitement. Whoever had converted what had originally been an Admiralty tender into a family cruiser might well have been catering for someone such as ourselves. In the bows were two separate cabins, each with two single bunks, next came a larger double cabin with an extra bunk above – opposite that was a very smart bathroom with three-quarter size bath and wash-basin and Calor gas water heater. Next came the saloon, with drip-feed oil heater and refrigerator and plenty of cupboard space: adjoining it a very practical galley with sink, gas cooker and more cupboard space. That was the fore-part of the boat: aft was yet another very large cabin with a double bed and two singles and, tucked behind a curtain, narrow bunks for two more if necessary! Finally, below deck, there was a really enormous engine room, so big that you could walk around it in comfort – the middle dominated by a gleaming Kelvin 88 h.p. diesel engine that looked well cared for, with a Lister generator at one side. Even then, the layout wasn't finished – for on deck level was a handsome wheel-house, with steering-wheel, ship to shore radio, echo sounder, etc., and behind that yet another deck cabin with two comfortable berths. In all there were five cabins to sleep thirteen people, plus a couple of extra narrow berths if necessary. She was more than a boat, she was a large family house on the water!

"Well," said Jess. "What do you think?"

I did in fact feel some genuine reservations, but I could hardly resist her enthusiasm. Then we both took a hard long look at the agents details again and came up against the formidable price asked: £6,000. Maybe it was not an unreasonable price, but it was far more than we could afford.

Jess looked around wistfully.

"You can always make an offer."

We drove all the way back to Cornwall, our minds filled with rosy images of what might be, and once home sat down and wrote, making an official offer. A few days later Laurent Giles's manager,

Commander Nicholls, replied more or less dismissing my offer out of hand, and that seemed that. Indeed, not long after we heard in a roundabout way that *Sanu* had been sold.

For a couple who had made up their minds to buy a boat and even had some financial means to do so, we seemed to be going round in circles. If I had thought more coherently about the matter I suppose I could have made approaches to some of the local fishermen over at Newlyn, one of whom might well have been prepared to sell off a fishing boat which we could get converted. On the other hand we knew nothing about conversions and little enough about boats – no, we felt it was more sensible to get a boat that was ready for use as a family cruiser.

Time passed. We made a few more abortive journeys and I went on conducting immense correspondence with agents and individuals all over Britain. I wish now I had kept some of those quite extraordinary and long letters which used to come out of the blue, extolling the virtues of this boat or that. And still, such were the powers of persuasiveness used, I was ready to go dashing off at a moment's notice – to Plymouth, to Bristol, to Lowestoft, to Milford Haven.

It was then that, out of the blue, I had an unexpected letter postmarked Worcester. Puzzled, I opened it to find several sheets covered in close hand-writing bringing to my attention the merits of a 50-ft. M.F.V. now lying at the basin at Worcester. She was powered by an Atlantic diesel engine, had very roomy accommodation, and as an example of her seaworthiness she had only recently returned from a voyage to the Channel Islands, France and Spain. As a matter of fact on the way out she had called in at St. Ives. . . .

Suddenly I remembered that time when I walked down the quay and saw the lovely white ship moored there – could it be? I hastily wrote off a postcard, and back came the answer. Yes, of course, this was M.F.V. *Batuba*. Wouldn't I like to come up and look her over?

For such a great believer in omens as myself that was practically enough: I felt that without a doubt we were meant to buy *Batuba*, otherwise why had I come upon her that memorable day? Jess was less dogmatic, but naturally interested, and we arranged a lightning visit to Worcester. Just before we went, almost as if she felt in some way she was behaving treacherously to her first love, Jess said:

"What about *Sanu* then?"

"Well, what about her? She's been sold."

"We don't know for certain, do we? I mean, it could have fallen through. Why don't you just write and make sure?"

I shrugged, but sent a query off to Laurent Giles: then we were on our way.

Early the next morning we were standing in the surprisingly large boat basin in Worcester, an unlikely spot I would have thought to have found such a centre.

Ah, yes, there was *Batuba*. I recognised her at once, even though on this wintry day she looked rather less white and shiny than in the summer at St. Ives. Her owner was waiting with that curious over-anxious air which exudes from all hoping to sell something. A part of me felt rather sorry for him, while another part kept thinking up cunning questions designed to ascertain the maximum information. Actually the tale that emerged was a rather sad, if ironic, one. For many years the owner had dreamed of having a boat, and finally had taken the plunge. He had persuaded his wife to agree to selling up their home and business and investing the money in *Batuba*, and with their two teenage sons off they had set on a two-year cruise. At first they enjoyed the change, and seeing new places like the Channel Islands and France, but then, after getting as far, I think, as San Sebastian, the romance began to wear off, particularly for the youngsters, who found one foreign port after another rather boring, and yearned increasingly for their familiar pals and girl friends. In the end there was nothing for it but to throw up the project and sail home again.

We believed the owner's story of why he was selling *Batuba*, we liked the general look of the boat, though finding her a little cramped by comparison with *Sanu*, and we were even half-tempted to make an offer there and then. But Jess was back to her old cautious self, so we arranged that we would come home, think it over, and give a definite decision within a couple of days.

"Well, what do you think?" I said as we neared home later that day.

"She's a nice boat. There's a lot to be said for her. It's only that—"

I grinned.

"You'd rather have *Sanu*?"

Jess nodded, but rather forlornly.

"Ah well, there'll be a letter from Laurent Giles when we get home and that will be that."

When we arrived there *was* a letter from Commander Nicholls, but not quite the one we had expected. For, it transpired, though a sale of *Sanu* had been fixed, at the last minute there had been an unexpected hitch and it had not gone through. The position was therefore that the boat was again on the market – would we care to make an offer?

Jess almost did a dance of joy, but I was sternly practical.

"Wait a minute – just *why* did the sale fall through, eh?"

The story of this was a complicated one, but in brief the prospective purchaser had not felt entirely happy about the condition of the boat – to offset this, Commander Nicholls explained, the owner of *Sanu* had arranged to get an independent survey, and if we were interested in the boat we could obtain a copy of this.

"Go on," said Jess, her eyes gleaming, "write for the survey."

"What about *Batuba*?"

"Well – let's wait till we see the survey."

There was a wait of another week or so, and then a bulky package arrived in the post. We had neither of us seen a survey before; this one was by a very reputable surveyor, and it was at once obvious that it was a fair and searching study of *Sanu*, from stem to stern. For us, of course, it made fascinating reading.

"The above yacht was surveyed while hauled out and also in the water. . . . The cabin sole was lifted as far as practicable; lockers were emptied and gear moved. Some lining in the saloon was removed and some skin fitting bolts were drawn. The structural members were tested by hammer and pricker.

"The yacht has been well maintained. She was built by a builder used to building this type of craft. She was built in the early part of the war when better materials were used than in later vessels of this type. This is confirmed by the very few defects that have been found. The hull is very strong and the scantlings are much in excess of Lloyds 100 A1 class."

The surveyor went on to deal item by item with no fewer than forty-eight parts of the boat. We read with growing confidence that the stem was hard both inside and out, that the keel was hard and in reasonably good condition, that the planking was good for the age of the vessel, that the rudder was satisfactory, the steering-gear in good working order, and that a number of other items – bollards, davits, rigging, masts and paintwork all passed inspection.

Finally the surveyor listed nine small defects that needed to be put right – a new plank under the forward passage, additional fastenings in one or two places, a renewal of some rails and bulwarks, and so on.

"If these defects are made good," he wrote, "then the yacht should have many more years of useful life ahead of her."

"Well," said Jess, "he recommends a number of repairs . . . the thing now is to get an estimate for these, and then make an offer taking them into account."

Which is what we did. This time, fairly obviously, having just lost a sale that seemed settled, the owner would be likely to be prepared to come down if there was a chance of another sale so quickly. Working on this assumption we settled down to the invariable period of postal haggling with Commander Nicholls,

until at last, one momentous day, our offer of £4,000 was accepted
— subject to the promise, on our part, that we should have a satisfactory engine test of *Sanu*. To this end I made yet another trip up
to Moody's boatyard for an appointment with the engineers, and
for the first time *Sanu* came really to life with the roaring and
pounding of the great Kelvin 88 horse-power diesel. Being of the
hand-starting variety it looked to me most formidable and frightening, even if the mechanic did swing it into action with just a
half-turn. I took the opportunity to get shown some of the other
mechanical devices of the boat, which all seemed equally baffling.
This was all very different from the neat modern diesel cruisers I
had taken on the rivers! On *Sanu* there were pipes and flexes running in all directions, complicated water systems and diesel stoves
— how would I ever understand them all?

Still, there it was, I had been given a satisfactory demonstration
of the engine, and there was nothing further to hold up the deal.
Of course there were all sorts of documents to be signed and
countersigned, and this all took time. At long last, however, the
deal was clinched, and one morning a fat, important looking enve-
lope arrived in the post — the ship's papers and legal history of
Sanu. We devoured the intimate pedigree with eager eyes.

"Official number, 186235: Registered 1955, Port of London,
No. 73; British single-screw motor ship, built at Looe, Cornwall,
in 1942, by F. Curtis and Co. Wooden Pleasure Yacht of carvel
build, with raked stem and cruiser stern. Number of masts, one,
number of decks, one, number of bulkheads, two . . ." And so on
and so on — there were the most intricate and obscure details, like
the number and diameter of the cylinders in the 88 horse-power
Kelvin engine, not to mention the 9 in. length of stroke and the
estimated 9 knots speed. Weights were given and broken down in
the most complicated way — there was 0·63 tons for the weight of
the aft cabin top, and 0·47 tons for "spaces for machinery and light
and air under Sect. 78 (2) of the Merchant Shipping Act, 1894" —
not to forget 2·66 tons for the bosun's store rooms! And on the

B

back of this formidable document (it measured about 2 feet long by 1 ft. across!) were the hand-written entries by the Customs and Excise clerks showing the previous transactions when ownership changed – one in 1960, and another later in the same year. Finally there was a new and up-to-date entry certifying that as from April 30th of that year, Denys Val Baker was the registered sole owner of the boat so described.

At long last I put down the papers and looked at Jess in some awe.

"We've got her – our very own boat!"

3

An Experience of Sea

For some days after becoming officially "the owner" I went about rather as a proud father does after hearing of the birth of a child: head in the air, eyes bright, and half-expecting everyone to come rushing up to congratulate me. Actually the idea of someone so generally impecunious as myself ever managing to own a boat was too much to stomach, and it soon became evident that our boat was regarded by our friends as something of a myth, and would be until we produced it in person. This we were anxious enough to do, but already, like any other child, *Sanu* was presenting us with all sorts of problems. She was not exactly a tiny wee thing to be wrapped up and put on a train or even a lorry, as is often done for the delivery of small boats. She was – and often I would repeat the figures in some awe to myself – a 60-ft. boat with a net weight of twenty-three tons. Getting this baby back home could be done one way only, and that was by sea.

But then there were other problems to be settled even before that one. Just *where* was our new baby to live? Apart from the fact we felt a little sensitive about how the St. Ives fishermen would react to our tyro efforts and wanted to acquire a professional touch before bringing *Sanu* to our home port, St. Ives was an unsuitable place in which to keep such a large boat permanently. We had lived there long enough to notice the often alarming and uncomfortable ground swell sea that came surging in, and which could quite easily lift a boat up and thump it down again with a resounding whack. Fortunately the ground surface is sand, but such

27

treatment cannot be too good for a boat over a long period – and in particular a large boat.

No, St. Ives would not qualify as a permanent berth. Then where? Now began several weeks of anxious inquiry and rejection which might have been amusing, if not rather serious from our point of view. First we set our sights on the inner harbour at Penzance, where the water level is kept up by closing the dock gates soon after high water. We had often noticed a cluster of half a dozen pleasure boats moored along the west quay – this would be a handy and apparently safe spot for *Sanu*, surely? But when we approached the harbour master we heard a different story. Oh, no, we wouldn't want to keep our boat there, why all manner of terrible things might happen – and then, don't forget, the big Trinity House steamers turned round, easy to get a bash. . . . In the end we allowed ourselves to be persuaded against, though to this day Penzance inner harbour always seems a tranquil and snug little home.

Next we tried Newlyn – after Brixham the West Country's biggest fishing port, a real honest-to-goodness fishing centre, sheltering sometimes as many as fifty or sixty large fishing vessels. I have always admired Newlyn and still do, but found that my own feelings counted for little – the idea of a purely pleasure boat of the size of *Sanu* settling in Newlyn was immediately frowned on heavily. This is understandable really, in a busy fishing port, but very sad again from our point of view, as I can think of no more pleasant haven. At least later on we were able to pay fleeting visits and enjoy the delightful experience of standing on board our boat at night-time and seeing all the lights of Newlyn twinkling around us.

Still, there it was : time was marching on, the baby was waiting to be delivered – where, oh where? We scanned the coastal map of Cornwall, excluding Hayle because of the bar there which restricted entry to high tide, considering in turn such tiny centres as Mousehole and Porthleven – and then finally coming to what then seemed the obvious choice: Falmouth, one of the finest natural estuaries in the world. Yes, we felt at once, Falmouth was the obvious place. True it was some twenty-odd miles away from us, but this should not prove too much of an obstacle – and just think of the advantages. It should be possible at Falmouth to have a deep-water berth, we would be in the centre of an area specialising in catering for boats, and what was more we would be well placed for all kinds of short exploratory cruises up and down the south coast.

So over to Falmouth we went, as ever feeling a curious thrill on coming round the bend in the road that suddenly reveals such a glorious view from Greenbank over the wide harbour front to Flushing and beyond. Almost everywhere one could see boats bobbing at anchor, from the massive Falmouth tugs that guide in ocean liners to the docks down to little fifteen-foot yachts.

"Well, *Sanu* would be snug enough here," I said. "But it looks quite crowded to me."

And so it was. When we inquired from the Falmouth Harbour Master about mooring space we found that the only vacant parts left for a boat of our size was a rather exposed stretch out by Trefusis Point on the Flushing side, a spot which would involve quite a long dinghy ride every time we wanted to get to the boat. In addition, to lay the kind of mooring necessary would cost us about £50. Since we could not be sure that we would always want to remain at Falmouth this seemed something of a commitment.

We decided that for the first season we might do better to rent an existing mooring, and here we were lucky. When we called on the Falmouth Boat Construction Company we found their manager, Mr. Thomas, most helpful, and he agreed to rent us a heavy mooring not fifty yards off shore from the boatyard, and very handy to the firm's fuelling pontoon.

"Just let us know what day you'll be arriving," said Mr. Thomas, "and we'll be on the look-out."

Now it was time to face the task of bringing *Sanu* round from Moody's boatyard at Swanwick Shore, near Southampton, to Falmouth. Not an easy trip, for it involved nearly 200 miles' travel along a coastline that could be pretty rough, especially as early in the season as April.

It wasn't only the weather that worried us either: while by now on our various river and canal trips, I had acquired a fair grasp of handling motor cruisers I did not feel in any way competent to bring *Sanu* round by sea on my own. Besides, even if I had felt like chancing it navigation-wise, so to speak, there remained the massive mystery of that Kelvin engine, the mere sight of which put the fear of God into a non-mechanical type like myself.

"I know what we can do on the engineering side," I said with sudden inspiration. "I'll ask Doug if he'd like to come."

Doug Rowe was in fact an agricultural diesel engineer whom we had met about a year previously at a time when a group of us thought seriously of starting a community out in New Zealand. The project had petered out, but we had kept in touch with Doug. We knew that his hobby was skin diving and that he spent much of his time pottering about on boats—and as I expected, when I made my proposition, he reacted with enthusiasm.

"I'll do my best with the Kelvin. Can you lend me the engine manual for a few days?"

Silently I handed over the thirty-six page instruction book on "The Running and Repairing of Model K" with its 120 separate detailed paragraphs, many of which at that stage read to me as comparative double-dutch, with such sentences as "It is preferable to bed the bush to a mandrel which is oversize by the amount of the clearance". At that early stage of my initiation to the world of *Sanu* I felt quite bewildered by all this jargon, but it was obviously all common sense to Doug, and I felt a great relief to know someone competent would be looking after the engine.

But what about the actual handling of the boat? Doug had already asked me, a little nervously, was I thinking of bringing her

down myself—and I had been amused to see the look of relief flooding his anxious face when I made it clear I intended to get someone more experienced to take charge. But just who? I had not previously mixed very much with the St. Ives fishermen or I might have been able to make arrangements with one of them. On the other hand I would have been a little nervous of getting so early involved with someone local in case later on we might not see eye to eye, and things might have become embarrassing. No, all in all it seemed most sensible to hire the services of someone who was a complete stranger, but of course professional at the job.

We began scanning the columns at the back of *Motor Boat and Yachting*, where firms advertise offering to deliver boats. I wrote off to two or three and finally settled—following a long and friendly phone chat during which his practical knowledge and enthusiasm impressed me—on Geoff Scott of Salcombe. His terms of £12 10s. per 100 miles, plus expenses, struck me, in all the circumstances, as reasonable.

Awaiting our particular B-Day I think both Jess and I were secretly terrified. She for her part had never really imagined that all our dreaming would so alarmingly turn into concrete fact and now found the reality a little overwhelming. I was less overwhelmed by the fact of owing a large boat—after all in our time we have owned some pretty strange objects from a seventeen-roomed vicarage to an old London taxi, and a 61-ft. boat somehow fitted in with the rest. No, what induced a nightmarish state of mind in me was the actual contemplation of the voyage down, with all its hypothetical problems. Being a man of a certain amount of creative imagination it was not difficult for me to conjure up the visions. Indeed, I would sit at my desk, supposedly writing a new story, in fact doodling horrific images of us in the *Sanu* going down stern first, or Jess and I swept off by a Channel gale—of the engines broken down and the boat drifting on to jagged rocks—oh, of all manner of terrible calamities. But then I was to find that, at sea as in other spheres, this was how I worked—going through all the alarming possibilities beforehand, and then being comparatively calm and collected at the actual time.

Our children, of course, were almost as excited as we were, though Stephen, aged 14, was most disconsolate that we would not allow him to stay away from school and make the trip. Now I am rather sorry that we didn't, but at the time the exclusion was made for a very well-meant reason – namely, just in case *Sanu* and all her crew foundered at sea!

As the date fixed drew nearer it seemed that all other matters faded into insignificance, we were so busy preparing ourselves for what, I am ashamed to remember, we obviously regarded as our ordeal. Jess was busy arranging for her pottery business to tick over and for someone to move in and look after the children, while I was in constant touch with Moody's, getting various checks made on the engine, and ordering in supplies of food.

At last the great day arrived. One of Jess's assistants in her pottery, Jackie Van Gelder, had decided to come along at the last moment, so when we assembled at seven in the morning to catch the train from St. Ives to Southampton there were four of us. Jess and I, Jackie and Doug – the latter bearing a heavy case of tools! It was a rather typical blustery rainy April day, but we tried not to notice the weather as the train sped on and on up country. *En route* we were joined by Geoff Scott, a reassuring figure in yachting cap and with a brown sun-tanned face and air of confidence.

Soon after four o'clock that afternoon we pulled into Moody's yard. It was not the best of moments, perhaps, for there was quite a strong wind buffeting the boats about and when the old boat man ferried us out to *Sanu* he murmured, "It's worse than it's been all winter". Certainly I would not have fancied the task of getting *Sanu* off her fore and aft moorings in the middle of that very narrow channel with boats moored round – but to Geoff, we soon found, this was just a matter of mathematics. He had us up at either end of the boat tightening and loosening ropes, and soon, despite the difficulties of wind and current our boat (which now

B*

we were in it seemed massive, like a passenger ship) had swung round and was heading down the River Hamble towards the Solent and the open sea.

We were off! Jess and I looked at one another in surprised excitement, especially as we came out of the narrow confines of the Hamble into the broad sweep of Southampton Water and found *Sanu* mingling with ocean liners and huge new oil boats. So far everything had worked out more satisfactorily than I could have dared to hope. The enormous Kelvin diesel with its rather complicated form of starting on petrol and switching over to diesel (and hand-starting at that) had functioned perfectly, as had the diesel generator. Coming down the river the boat sat in the water as steady as a rock, and even now that we were passing down towards the Isle of Wight in quite a heavy swell she rode the waves beautifully. The wind that threatened had not so far worsened, and since we knew we were only bound another ten miles or so for Yarmouth we felt we could relax. Indeed, all five of us christened our voyage there and then with nips from a bottle of rum bought specially for the occasion. Just as darkness was falling we came into Yarmouth Harbour, a snug and cosy place for a boat.

After pouring over charts and tide tables we decided, on Geoff's strong advice, to make a very early start in the morning in order to obtain six hours of tide in our favour, to balance six hours against, for our comparatively long journey from Yarmouth to Brixham, in Devon. On the smooth paper of the charts this trip, though about ninety miles, looked feasible for a sturdy M.F.V. that could average seven knots, but no sooner had we left Yarmouth soon after dawn than Geoff tuned in to the weather forecast and got a warning of Force 6 to 7, which even types like Jess and I knew to be not at all healthy. At almost the same time, our skipper pointed to one or two quite large cargo boats ordered off the shore and explained that they were lying up to wait for better weather.

"What would you like to do? My job is to deliver boats and I just push on, but it might be quite rough. It's up to you."

We looked at one another doubtfully.

"If it's the boat you're worrying about, stop worrying," said Geoff cheerfully. "I'd go in this boat anywhere, round the world if need be. And I would not be worried if I were caught in a gale, she'd ride out anything."

I suppose it was impossible for *Sanu*'s new owners to resist such insidious flattery. Feeling a great warm glow of well-being, we ignored the cowering cargo boats and the ominous distant white-caps on the waves out in the open sea beyond the Needles.

"Oh, we'll carry on, of course."

It wasn't long before we were to regret those airy instructions. No sooner had we passed beyond the Needles than the whole nautical climate seemed to change. Whereas we had been heading fairly steadily through regular swells, now we were suddenly bat-tering against large, choppy and changeable seas. *Sanu*, large and heavy though she was, began to toss about like a cork, pitching up and down and, more ominously, rolling too. The effect upon the crew was slow but deadly. Geoff, of course, seasoned seaman that he was, remained unaffected. Doug took immediate evasive action against what possibly might "come upon him" by leaving the wheel-house and retiring to the stern of the boat – quite a risky journey as we were tossing about at alarming angles. For the next three hours we never saw or heard from him again, and even began to worry, with visions of him having disappeared overboard in one of the extra big rolls. . . . However, when Geoff finally went to have a look he found Douglas curled up asleep on the stern deck. Ever afterwards Douglas clung firmly to the very sensible belief that in rough seas it is healthier by far to be in the fresh open air. The rest of us were less fortunate on that first momentous day. Jess was the first to become strangely quiet in one corner of the wheel-house, at last silently but urgently beckoning me to pass a bucket. Shortly after, Jackie retired rather hastily to her cabin below and remained there for the rest of what was to prove a very rough trip. Up in the wheel-house, standing beside

Geoff and sharing with him the steering of the boat, I felt reasonably confident. Hadn't I just recently survived two or three very rough crossings on the River Shannon? Hadn't I been unscathed through trips to France and to the Channel Isles and, even worse, the Scilly Isles? I had indeed; but no amount of self-bolstering could ward off the clammy feeling spreading over me. At last, at precisely the same moment that Jess decided to be sick again, I, too, had to grab for a bucket. Whereupon Jess and I experienced a new but rather traumatic "sharing" experience of married life— crouched together side-by-side being sick into buckets!

As it happened we weren't putting up such as bad show as, guiltily, we felt. Geoff admitted the conditions were pretty bad and that if we hadn't been anxious to get on with the journey he might well have hesitated himself. In the end, when the tide had turned against us and the trip to Brixham still involved a further fifty miles or so, he suggested that it might be a good idea to pull in at Weymouth and call it enough for that day. Needless to say, we all agreed wholeheartedly! As soon as we came up to Weymouth the sea calmed down and we were thus able to enjoy our first entry into a large port. We felt very important chugging up to the harbour entrance—until suddenly men in uniform scurried about and two red flags were hoisted, which meant we had to turn round hastily and get clear—just as well, for almost immediately there appeared the enormous prow of the cross-Channel steamer bound for Guernsey and Jersey, its deck lined with grinning passengers.

"Just wait till they get out to sea," said Geoff, with some satisfaction, "they won't be grinning then."

Once inside Weymouth Harbour we soon recovered our spirits and wolfed an enormous meal. Meantime, we were listening anxiously to weather forecasts for the next twenty-four hours. They didn't sound very hopeful, but Geoff was an incurable optimist and kept assuring us that the next day would be less rough.

Fractionally he may have been right, but there wasn't much in it. The only improvements were (*a*) that we had got our sea legs and weren't sick again; (*b*) the sun shone brightly the whole ten hours or so of the sixty-three miles journey from Weymouth across Lyme Bay and round Start Point to Salcombe. It was quite an experience, too, for us, beginning with a short-cut journey inside the renowned Portland Race, and including periods when we were so far out at sea as to lose sight of land altogether.

This time, once the boat was set on her course, we left Geoff in the wheel-house and the four of us sat at the stern of the boat. It really was a wonderful experience, with the boat steadily riding up and down the quite large swells. The sea wasn't as choppy as the previous day, but the rise and fall of the waves was sometimes quite extraordinary to our unfamiliar eyes – to be sitting at the back and feel yourself suddenly high up in the air, perhaps twenty feet up, and then come crashing down again was quite marvellous. In particular, I found this an excellent training in handling *Sanu*, and by the time we came in sight of Salcombe Harbour I felt quite the skipper – until Geoff began talking about the jagged rocks that lie across part of the entrance! However, we managed to anchor safely enough at Salcombe, and early the next morning, soon after seven o'clock in fact, we were off again on the last leg of our trip. We would have started even earlier but *Sanu*, we discovered, was equipped with possibly one of the heaviest anchors ever carried by a boat of her size! It needed all the combined efforts of three of us to bring it up again.

At last we were heading across Plymouth Bay, and soon the unmistakable needle point of Eddystone Lighthouse could be seen clearly on the horizon. This, our last and third day, saw a complete change in weather. The sea, previously so unpleasant, became relatively calm, and we really began to enjoy our cruise as it should be, sitting in the sun, inspecting passing craft, following the outline of the coast – Rame Head, Gribbin Head, Dodman Point. Soon, a little too confidently, Doug and I thought we saw the entrance to Falmouth, but it was, in fact, a cove some ten miles before. At last there was no mistaking the landmarks, and at about 2.30 on a fine sunny afternoon the M.F.V. *Sanu*, skippered by Geoff Scott of Salcombe, and most cheerfully crewed by the rest of us, came round St. Antony Head and travelled at reduced speed up the Carrick Roads and into Falmouth harbour.

There was one last moment of amusing confusion. Mr. Thomas had told me to look out for a small red mooring buoy — when we reached the appointed spot there were six red mooring buoys almost in a row! However, we sorted this out, put over the boat-hook and pulled up the buoy, quickly pulled in the chain and firmly and securely moored *Sanu* to her new base.

For the last time on that trip, Doug shut off the valiant Kelvin engine which had beat away steadily without faltering, and we all clambered out on deck. It was a lovely spring afternoon, sunlight falling on the sheer waters of Falmouth harbour lighting up the dozens of boats moored there: tugs, fishing boats, yawls, sloops, racing yachts, even the old schooner *Falcon*, newly arrived from Penzance after an equally rough trip — and behind the green and yellow fields of Flushing rising up to the skyline. It was a lovely, heartening sight and, waiting for us in the future, lay the way to the open sea.

4

The Seventh Child

From the moment we deposited *Sanu* at her permanent mooring at Falmouth that spring our whole way of life seemed to change (I don't know whether to say radically or alarmingly!) For Jess and I there was a new kind of overhanging worry, a niggling anxiety. Is *she* all right? Will the chain hold? Did we shut off the sea cock? What about the Calor gas? Are all the portholes closed? I am inclined to worry anyway, and in those early weeks of boat-ownership I think I must have exceeded all previous records. Time after time, especially on a wild and stormy night, I would start awake and think fearfully about my new charge, perhaps rocking violently in the middle of Falmouth Harbour with nothing between her and destruction but a big red mooring buoy and chain. Oh, if only we could have kept her somewhere nice and handy, where we could keep an eye on the poor old thing!

For the children, of course, the change was a more pleasant and exciting one, and they were impatient to celebrate.

"We want to see the boat! When are we going to see the boat?"

After four hectic days at sea with *Sanu* neither Jess nor I minded a brief respite but two days after our return I took pity on the children and we drove them over for, so to speak, a ceremonial introduction. Secretly I was as proud as any father showing off his new infant, so I was naturally flattered when, after we came in view of the harbour and I pointed out *Sanu*, there were gasps of disbelief and astonishment.

"Not *that* one? Why it's the biggest in the harbour."

41

This was a slight exaggeration, but all the same *Sanu* was one of the largest, overshadowed only by the large sea-going tugs that moored in rows down the centre lane.

When we had left *Sanu* we had rowed to the pontoon in our fibreglass dinghy, which was waiting there now for us, bobbing gently in the afternoon swell. Stephen looked momentarily disappointed at seeing no outboard, but cheered up when I explained that there was a 15 horse-power Gale engine on *Sanu* which as yet we hadn't got around to fitting up on the dinghy. He clambered excitedly into the front of the dinghy and Jess sat at the back with a slightly more nervous Demelza and Genevieve, and I rowed the family sedately out to their new acquisition.

From the roadway *Sanu* had looked large enough, but now, approaching by dinghy, she looked enormous, like some ocean-going liner. I can still remember now the slight feeling of awe that came over me as I looked over my shoulder to make sure I was heading right for the ladder steps which we kept fixed over the side. Was this *really* our boat – our very own?

Once aboard, the children ran off on an excited tour of inspection, with Jess and I following more slowly. It was a pleasant occasion, the first time the whole family had been on board together – precursor one vaguely sensed, of so many other times. Jess and I sat on the flat aft cabin rooftop at the back listening to the children's excited cries as they made one discovery after another. One of the unexpected features of *Sanu* was that she was fairly well stocked with all sorts of useful items, such as life-belts, oilskins, flags, caps, torches, lamps, many of which we now unearthed tucked away in cupboard and drawers. More enticing still from the children's point of view there was quite a handsome haul of food stocks put away in the galley for emergencies – though I don't think they were especially attracted to the largest single haul, seventeen tins of creamed rice!

Almost as if by instinct the children took over the large aft cabin as their headquarters, which is what Jess and I had in mind anyway. Apart from the saloon this was the largest cabin on the boat and would, in its original version, have been the crew's main sleeping quarters. During our inspection of various other fishing boats I noted that most of them had this kind of rear quarters. Some indeed had quite extensively planned cabins, with bunks let into the sides in double rows, providing sleeping accommodation for as many as eight people. Ours was not quite on that scale, but something similar in style – on the right side, or as I now began to remember to call it, the starboard side, there was a large double berth, and behind that, that is nearer to the stern, ran a single berth – while on the opposite, port side, there was another single berth. In addition there was room for a diesel-oil-burning stove, a washbasin, a Calor gas water-heater and several rows of large cupboards and drawers. The aft cabin was very light and airy, too, for the whole of the centre ran under a large double glass canopy through which Jess and I now peered with amusement watching the scurrying forms of the children. However they soon learned that if they wanted privacy they could easily hang one of the red curtains right across and then indulge in all kinds of secret sessions. On later occasions the aft cabin thus became a gambling saloon, a gang headquarters and something of a necking parlour.

But principally, of course, the pleasures of *Sanu* were those of what she represented – the sea. Merely to be aboard her, even in the comparative calm of Falmouth Harbour, was to be aware of immense potentialities. Even if these could not be immediately explored, there were other minor pleasures of the same kind. Soon Stephen and I between us had unearthed the Gale outboard, cleaned it up and then, using the davits, lowered it gingerly down into the dinghy. Stephen swarmed down the ladder and fixed the engine securely to the transom and, as it was a lovely spring afternoon, we decided to take a little outing. Unlike so many outboard engines I have observed spluttering and faltering, this one started at a touch and in no time at all we were zooming around the considerable environs of Falmouth Harbour, weaving in and out of the moored yachts, visiting the big dockyards and then over to Flushing, finally travelling back down the deep channel at quite a speed. After that, of course, the outboard journeys became one of Stephen's delights, especially when he realised that the engine was a very powerful one and that, when in the dinghy alone, he could achieve quite high speeds – a tendency which finally I had to curb harshly after receiving complaints from other boat owners about the wash being created!

The children were obviously thrilled with *Sanu* and we promised that it wouldn't be long before we took them to sea. In the meantime, however, we needed time to get to know this big lusty new infant of ours, and so we arranged with our friend Doug to spend a whole day aboard getting to know the innards more painstakingly than had been possible on the trip down. While Jess began a big clean out and reorganisation of the galley, Doug and I plunged down into the mysterious depths of *Sanu*'s engine room. Unlike the engine rooms on many other boats we had viewed, this one proved to be exceptionally roomy, stretching the whole width of eighteen feet across, and being about fifteen feet long, with plenty of head room. Dead in the centre, not unlike some goddess statue awaiting worship, rested the Kelvin 88 horse-power engine – a huge iron monster whose total weight was about four tons, much of it now hidden below the floor boards. The part which rose up above, crowned with shining brass piston tops and gleaming copper piping, always seemed to me to have a beauty of its own. I am sure that this is how it seemed to Doug, with his engineering appreciation, for he immediately got down to it with Brasso and grease and had the engine room all shiny and glowing in no time. In between times he tried to impart to me some knowledge of diesel engineering – not at that time very successfully, I fear, for I was terrified of the whole contraption. However, determined to avoid complete ignominy, I managed to master the small $3\frac{1}{2}$ horse-power Lister generator engine, which started fairly easily with a turn of the handle. This in turn charged up the four six-volt batteries which, wired to give a twenty-four-volt supply, provided *Sanu* with its electricity system. It was really quite impressive how extensive this system was. Every cabin had at least one electric light, some even had two and the saloon had six. In addition there was a small electric refrigerator, and a converter which enabled the use of such gadgets as a vacuum cleaner or even a television set! At that romantic stage the idea of watching television on a boat seemed perfectly ludicrous, but I suppose if one was making very long journeys in the open sea it might break the monotony.

Now it was the turn of Doug and myself to experience the children's excitement of discovering things. We began emptying drawers and cupboards in the engine room and unearthing a formidable collection of spare parts: washers, springs, valves, piston rings, injectors — even a complete fuel filter system.

"My word," said Doug. "That's probably worth £50."

At first I felt rather thrilled at this apparent gain, but soon my pleasure was dampened as I began to experience the reality of that well-known adage, boats are expensive things. We didn't exactly intend *Sanu* as a plaything, but still she now proved expensive.

First, there were the repairs that just had to be done. For instance, we realised that our batteries simply weren't holding their charges and this meant really that we had to get four new batteries. But these were nothing like the ordinary car batteries I was used to buying at about £4 each — these were special heavy duty batteries, the cheapest of which was nearly £12 each, making a total outlay of just under £50 at once. Next we found we had to get a new dynamo regulator, another £18-odd. Then it turned out that there was a faulty valve in our ship-to-shore radio, and the aerial needed attention, while the echo sounder also had to be adjusted. One way and another on the electric side alone we had to spend nearly £150 before we were finished. Still, I kept telling myself, it was better to get these things fixed in the beginning.

Next there was the question of improvements. One small but what I felt very necessary item which I had put in hand at once was the provision of a pair of stout wooden legs. These are devices used by most deep keel boats to ensure that if caught in a harbour that dries out they won't heel over but can lean against a harbour wall. You can with the right foresight lean against a harbour wall without a leg, by running a rope from the mast ashore, but it is not a method really to be recommended, and a leg saves a lot of worry.

At the time I was considering having legs made I was surprised at the vehemence with which one or two yachting friends pooh-poohed the idea, saying they would just "be a damn nuisance and get in your way". The fact is that our legs have never got in the way, and they have proved invaluable. Through Falmouth Boat Yard I ordered two legs to be made of strong Canadian elm. When they were finally delivered, after being measured and shaped to fit the boat, I must admit I was a little taken aback at their size. For a boat like *Sanu*, weight twenty-three tons, the legs had to be really solid, and the ones we had were so heavy that we found three men were needed to lift one up. This was a nuisance, but subsequently when we were visiting innumerable spots where the tide washed away leaving us high and dry I have often been grateful for our huge wooden legs.

At the back of our minds Jess and I had ideas for several interior improvements, particularly to the saloon, but we decided to leave these till the end of our first season. Exteriorwise, however, we knew one job that had to be done at once, and that was to give *Sanu* a fresh coat of paint. At the time we acquired her she was a strange conglomeration of light blue and navy blue, green and cream, not a very appetizing mixture. We discovered later that she had originally been light blue and white which must have been a more pleasing combination, but the present effect we did not like.

So, bright and early one May morning, Doug and Jess and I rowed out to *Sanu* bearing with us several tins of new paint – black for the hull, and white for the tops of the cabin and wheel-house, and a supply of dekaplex to put over the deck.

At first the job was not too difficult, since we just went round the deck painting the bulwarks and a foot or two below that. Then came the testing time — nothing for it but to pile into the dinghy and start painting the hull from the water. Not such an easy job as it may sound, even in calm water. We took it in turns, one of us remaining on *Sanu* to look after the rope of the dinghy and move it along whenever needed — the other two, each armed with a paint brush and tin, standing on the dinghy and painting a section of the hull at a time. Needless to say, progress was somewhat haphazard: twice Doug nearly fell into the water, though once it was the fault of the Flushing ferryboat passing too near with its big wash. On another occasion Jess lost her paint tin into the water . . . one way and another I am afraid Falmouth Harbour was not any cleaner for our efforts. However, the worst sufferer was our lovely spotlessly white dinghy which soon began to look as if it had black and white spotted fever.

Still . . . we *were* getting on with the job. Gradually, section by section, *Sanu*'s enormous navy blue hull changed into a rich glossy black. It was a job that could very well take a week to accomplish professionally, whereas we finished it off in a couple of concentrated, if slightly amateurish, days. At least, blemishes and all, we did achieve our immediate objective. Apart from painting the hull we had also painted the top structure white, and the effect was to bring down the height of the wheelhouse and make *Sanu*'s proportions altogether more pleasing. It was with real pride that we turned to take a last look that evening — it really was almost like seeing another boat altogether.

Soon our regular presence among the boats at Falmouth brought us into contact with other boat owners. Vernon Rose, who like us lived in St. Ives but kept a cutter over at Falmouth, came aboard one day to have a look round — so did one or two other friends with boating experience. Everyone was so obviously impressed with the sheer solidity and obvious seaworthiness of *Sanu* that I suppose gradually I began to relax some of my original fears. This,

of course, was before we embarked on any sea voyages! I did not
even allow my equilibrium to be unduly disturbed when a rather
tattered looking *Falcon* schooner settled nearby, shortly after her
devastating experience of setting out from Penzance to Gibraltar
and losing her mast in a storm in the Bay of Biscay. Several friends
of ours had been on the *Falcon* at the time and we had heard hair-
raising stories of the mast falling overboard and threatening to
take the boat as well—but thanks to the ability of George, the
skipper and owner, the *Falcon* had managed to return. Well, I
told myself, these hazards await every ship. The main thing was
that a boat like *Falcon*, and I felt sure a boat like *Sanu*, was built
to weather such situations.

And indeed, looking back on those early days of "getting to
know you" at Falmouth, I remember most this sense of real
confidence in the boat's enduring qualities. After all, those four
days of bringing her down had not only taught us a good deal of
general seamanship they had demonstrated more strikingly than
any words just how tough a craft *Sanu* was. Now, browsing
among a mass of old papers we found in various drawers on the
board we came across some interesting early log books, dating back
to the Admiralty period, from which we had a rather endearing
picture of *Sanu*'s days of humdrum service, when obviously she
had been used as a sort of general tender boat.

Obviously, we could imagine, such a life might have proved
rather dull, except at the end when apparently *Sanu* was used for
carrying explosives out to be dumped in the English Channel. So
probably the old girl was not sorry when finally she was sold for
conversion into a private cruiser.

This was about the first time that I paid any real attention to
Sanu's less immediate antecedents. When we received a mass of
documents at the time of finally acquiring legal ownership these
included the earlier bills of sale and so forth. Now looking idly
through these I found that prior to the previous owner, Commander Pirie, of the Outward Bound School, *Sanu* had had two

other owners, and then before them the original owner who had carried out the conversion. His name, I now read, was Dorrien David Saqui. . . . Wait, wasn't there something rather familiar about that? Of course! David Saqui was the name of the former husband of a friend of ours in St. Ives, someone we had actually met only a couple of years ago. He now lived in Fowey, where he ran a restaurant, but we remembered hearing that before then he had a boat—took people shark fishing.

"Coincidence is a strange thing," murmured Jess.

"Yes, indeed," I agreed. "Well, we must have a long talk with David—it'll be great help to hear from him about *Sanu*'s original appearance and so on."

We were in fact to have an opportunity before long to have such a talk with David, though in circumstances of slight humiliation. But more of that in the next chapter. For the time being we went on searching through our papers and discovering old charts which suggested that *Sanu* had travelled quite wide afield—as far apparently as Norway in the north, and down the coast of Brittany in the south. At this stage the prospect of such journeys remained very much in the realms of myth for Jess and I, and we stared at these scraps of evidence with marvelling eyes. It hardly seemed credible that one day again, but this time bearing us with her, *Sanu* should sail off to such regions.

At least, sitting at home in my office looking out on Porthmeor Road and mundane daily activities, it seemed incredible. But often, sitting aboard *Sanu* under a blue sky, surrounded by yachts with sails filling out, watching a passing motor cruiser or some schooner—finding almost every day some new arrival moored nearby, such as the *Falcon*, or a tiny 17-ft. yacht from the Hebrides —then, indeed, the mythical seemed more real. And perhaps most of all in the early evening, when dusk had fallen, and the water was alive with the glittering lights of the houses along the harbour front, and of the boats gliding backwards and forwards. Then one had an even greater sense of suppressed excitement, as we dared to contemplate days when we would be sitting in *Sanu* not merely in the safety of Falmouth, but in the unfamiliarity of other even more exotic ports.

So we began to prepare for our first family outing in *Sanu*. We had painted the exterior of the boat, and some of the interior. We had cleaned and repainted the deck; downstairs we had taken down the partition from the galley, incorporating it into a rather larger and more convenient saloon. We had sorted out all the cutlery and crockery and other odds and ends, and bought in any extra stocks necessary. Naturally, since Jess was a potter, we scorned to buy any crockery — instead, she made a set of tall mugs especially for the boat, and also brought along one or two useful jugs and bowls. We took home all the sheets and blankets and covers and washed and cleaned them all ready for "the season". At the same time we brought over quite a stock of tinned foods to add to what was there already, so that when setting off on a voyage all we needed to get beyond was fresh foods such as milk, bread and butter and meat.

Meantime Doug and I were checking up on the mechanical side of things. Owing to the fact that he lived near Falmouth and was working elsewhere most of the time our meetings did not always coincide and this led one day to consternation. I came aboard the boat and glacing casually at the fuel indicators saw that we were over 100 gallons short of diesel fuel. This was such an extra-ordinary fact that I was quite flabbergasted. At first, in my usual neurotic fashion I imagined there was a leak, and went round sniffing for oil — then the absurdity struck me, for if there were 100 gallons of diesel oil loose in the boat I would have noticed at once!

Not unnaturally, I began to suspect larceny, especially after I learned from the pontoon foreman that such things were not un-known in a busy harbour like Falmouth. Fortunately just as I was on the point of going to the police and imagined getting involved in all manner of dreary inquiries, Doug came along and it transpired that he had forgotten to reconnect the gauges after we had filled up.

This was the kind of alarum to which I am unhappily prone. In a car I listen for every minute deviation in the rattlings and can sense something going wrong even before it happens. Jess gets angry about this and says I "will" things to go wrong. However that may be, I now found the same tendencies with *Sanu*. I was always convinced when I first saw her from the bank that she had a list to one side, or that her bow was "down" at the front. Once aboard, I was always hearing strange noises and creaks full of ominous intents.

Fortunately, the rest of my family are less superstitious, and so with the help of their healthy scepticism I managed to avoid giving way to the worst of my fantasy fears. Two weeks after we brought *Sanu* down to Falmouth I had to admit, a little apprehensively, that she was now finally and irrevocably ready for her first outing in the combined charge of myself at the wheel and Doug Rowe at the engine.

5

The Week-end Voyagers

LOOKING back, the almost excruciating nervousness with which we approached our first outing in *Sanu* may seem out of proportion; but then one is always alarmed by the unknown. Although in fact we travelled down from Southampton in *Sanu* in conditions as bad as any we might expect to encounter we did so under the benevolent care of a sort of father-figure, our skipper Geoff Scott. When we felt unwell we were able to go and sit miserably in a quiet corner, safe in the knowledge that Geoff was at the wheel — good old Geoff would see things through! Now it was going to be alarmingly different!

Not that I had been neglecting my duties as skipper-navigator. As soon as we bought *Sanu* I embarked on an intensively busy relationship with Imray and Wilson Ltd., a London firm specialising in supplying charts and navigational books. Already my desk was cluttered up with *Reed's Almanac*, that bible of the amateur sailor; *The Channel Pilot*, Volume 1; *Motor Boat and Yachting Manual*; *Yachtman's and Boatowner Handbook*; and a variety of fascinating technical books with titles like *At Home in Deep Waters* and *Yacht Repairs and Conversions*. Now I decided to get in a very full supply of charts covering the Western Channel areas, with particular reference to Cornwall. First I got those godsends to yachtsmen, the coloured maps put out by Edward Standford and Co., of which I cannot speak too highly. Here in simple form is presented all the main information needed by small-boat navigators. Stanford's even lay down the lines and courses for most of the main journeys likely to be made on any particular stretch of coast. I remembered a friend of mine who had once brought a boat round from London saying enthusiastically, "It's just like having an AA route!"

All the same I realised there might be dangers in relying too much on set courses, so in addition to the Standford Chart of the Western Channel I decided to buy the relevant Admiralty Charts. Here I found I was taking on quite a problem, for the Admiralty Charts, even covering the Cornish coastlines, total more than thirty! Full of enthusiasm I ordered most of them, including some fascinating large-scale charts of such small areas as Falmouth Harbour, Plymouth Sound, the Scilly Isles, Penzance Bay and Fowey Harbour.

Now our attendance at navigational classes began to pay dividends, for Jess and I found it (on paper at least!) comparatively simple to plot courses up and down the coast, after making due allowances for deviation and variation. Apart from the actual plotting I found a growing interest in making a really close study of the actual chart and finding out item by item where every important marking was, buoys, lighthouses, lightships and so forth.

"Well," said Jess one evening as we sat with maps spread all over the floor. "Where shall we go to?"

I looked down at the coloured map and the winding twisting outline of the Cornish coast.

"The idea generally is that we'll make a series of trips to each of the main ports."

"Every week-end, you mean?"

"Yes." I hesitated, back to caution. "But for our first trip don't you think it would be a good idea to make it a fairly *short* one – a *day* trip to somewhere and back again?"

"Where to, then?"

I pondered over the map, working out distances, then turned to *Reed's Almanac* and checked on tides and harbour details . . . finally looking up triumphantly.

"How about to Mevagissey? That's about eighteen miles there and the same back — we should be able to do that comfortably."

Today a trip out of just over two hours would seem very small beer, but we approached this momentous first outing to Mevagissey with as much attention to detail as someone embarking on an ocean-going voyage. Several days beforehand I rang up the Mevagissey harbour master and ascertained that it would be possible to moor at the outer quay there, which would be free on a Sunday. I had already found out that while the inner harbour dried out there would be sufficient depth of water by the South Pier so that we should be quite comfortable for mooring. My last remaining Scorpion-cautious procedure, on the morning of the trip, was to ring up the coastguards at Mevagissey and obtain a weather report — just to make sure there were no unforseen troubles, like an impending gale!

In case these precautions may seem rather profuse I must say even now that, with greater experience of the sea, I would not retract any of them. The sea and the weather are eternally restless and inclined to treachery, and every possible bit of foresight is valuable. In addition, it has to be remembered that our voyage was being made in a 61-ft. long boat whose proportions are such that it is cumbersome to handle and cannot necessarily go everywhere because of its draft.

At last the great day came, the first Sunday in May. By luck it was sunny and warm, and this greatly added to our good spirits. Doug Rowe had brought along his wife, Sheila, and their little daughter, Sharen, and some other friends of ours, Ken and Jane Moss and their small daughter, Abigail, had come over from Sennen, so our total complement numbered eleven.

Just before midday Doug and I went down to the engine room and began operations. The Kelvin is what is called a petrol-starting diesel: that is, there are four starting-plugs operating on petrol and these are fired first to get the diesel warmed up — then a lever is pulled which switches over to diesel. The main problem, it

seemed in those early days, was swinging the huge handle. I soon
found out in fact that it was a knack, merely requiring a half-turn
at the right point, but at first I was inclined to put trust in brute
strength, straddling the floor and bending down and heaving
furiously at the handle, until sweat was pouring down my fore-
head.

On paper, I must admit, starting our engine sounds a complicated process, for I made a list of the necessary preliminary procedures as follows: (1) Open sea-cock; (2) Remove magneto stopping-terminal from its pin; (3) put impulse starter into action by
tightening screw beside magneto; (4) Put reverse gear into neutral;
(5) Check governor lever in mid-position; (6) Turn change-over
valves to petrol; (7) Pour petrol into carburetter; (8) Prime cylinders with petrol–oil mixture; (9) Turn handle until engine fires;
(10) Wait few seconds then push change-over hand lever full forward and close injector drains; (11) Put impulse starter out of
action by slackening screw beside magneto; (12) Replace stopping-
pin in magneto; (13) Put sparking plugs out of action by placing
stopping-terminal on its pin. . . . However, I'm glad to say that in
practice all these processes became second nature and starting the
great engine, barring unforeseen problems, has become a matter
of a few minutes at most.

Fortunately there was no hitch on this particular Sunday. After
listening to the steady throb of power for a few moments Doug
gave a thumbs up signal, and I hurried up to take my post at the
wheel. Our next problem was to take a good look round at the
craft in our vicinity and make sure we were well clear of them
before releasing our grip on the mooring chain.

I lowered the window of the wheel-house and signalled to Doug
and Ken, who were standing forward by the anchor winch – with
a quick movement they freed the mooring chain and it ran back
into the water. I touched the throttle, pulling the wheel hard over
– and slowly, but with gathering speed, began to move. We were
off!

It was a curious moment of fulfilment as *Sanu* purred down the main channel out of Falmouth Harbour, past the long line of docks with their huge liners under repair. The children and the others were sitting or standing on the deck watching the passing panorama of other boats and widening water – and here was I standing at the wheel, solely responsible for boat and crew. The thought was a daunting one yet not as alarming as I had imagined, for it was impossible not to sense the power and purpose of *Sanu*, the confidence with which she ploughed out through the water. Soon we had left the docks and were passing parallel to Pendennis Castle, with the continental-looking resort of St. Mawes away on our left. Ahead of us was Black Rock, which I must keep to my starboard – and there, too, on our port stood the black and white building of St. Anthony Lighthouse, with which we were to become familiar as we made more and more trips.

I began to relax, as we headed out to sea and settled on a course of 265° for Dodman Point, as conveniently given by Stanford's. All around us the sun shimmered on the calm sea, here and there were little fishing boats or an odd motor speed-boat – on the horizon the smoke of one or two Channel steamers. Oh, this was very pleasant, very pleasant indeed.

I called out to Jess.

"Well. . . .?"

She grinned, waved – and went to take some ciné snaps.

One of the first things we learned on the trip down the coast was the eternal difficulty of correctly identifying the lay of the land. Fortunately after a few miles we came in sight of Gull rock, which rises 125 feet above the water near Penmore Head . . . and then the dark protruding Dodman Point. Both Gull and Dodman represented jagged stretches of ugly looking rocks, and we felt a lot happier when we had rounded the point. Now I had to make sure to keep well clear of Gwineas Rock, but since this was marked by a buoy this was simple enough.

We were getting near journey's end. After a momentary diver-

c

sion where some of us thought the rather similar looking port of Portmellon was our intended objective, we managed to identify Mevagissey, and I headed *Sanu* towards the South pier.

Now, of course, I was beginning to feel a little nervous. This would be the first time I had brought *Sanu* into a harbour, and Mevagissey — as I learned from furiously rereading the Channel Pilot beside me — was by no means an ideal one to enter. The South pier was at a steep angle to the North pier, and the aperture of entry was quite narrow. *Sanu*, with her 61 ft. length and 18 ft. beam, and her single engine, was hardly a boat that could be swung round abruptly: we had to think ahead and plot a fairly devious approach to come up by the quay.

A certain amount of tension now made itself felt aboard the good ship *Sanu*! Jess came beside me in case I needed reinforcing. Doug stood up front with a rope, and Ken went back with another rope, while Stephen also stood at the ready.

I took a last look round as we came nearer and nearer to the entrance.

"Slow down!" said Jess urgently.

"I was *about* to do that. But remember I mustn't slow down too much, or I shall lose control."

Sanu's pace reduced, but, if one looked at the approaching land-fall, hardly enough. I hesitated and then throttled down still more, but I remained rather worried about coming round the bend into the harbour. In the end, rightly I think, I made a wide sweep so that I could enter more or less in a straight line, and heading for the South quayside — which, I was relieved to see, was empty of other shipping.

"You're still going too fast," warned Jess.

"I can't help it, I must have some way on the ship."

"Well don't forget to reverse."

I had no intention of forgetting this important last minute manoeuvre in coming up to a berth — but I did rather omit to allow sufficient time for operating *Sanu*'s rather old-fashioned method of gear change, which consists of a hand wheel which has to be turned one full circle either clockwise or anti-clockwise, according to whether you want to go forward or backwards. In addition, in a moment of confusion, I could not quite remember which way one turned the hand wheel. . . . To cut a sad story short, though I throttled right down and did in the end get the gear into reverse, it was all, as Jess was acidly to point out, a little late, and our arrival at Mevagissey was celebrated by a resounding thud as our bow hit the harbour wall.

Fortunately the bang wasn't really a very bad one; and in any case it was forgotten in the face of an entirely new problem. We had come in on a rising tide, so that we knew we would be safe for depth for several hours, but the result was the harbour wall now seemed to tower some distance above us! Somehow we had envisaged coming alongside and someone stepping on to the quay and tying up our ropes. Now we found we were alongside the quay but somehow not of it, and there seemed to be no ladder or way of getting up. Meantime the boat was showing signs of wanting to slip away from the quay.

I watched in irritated impotence as Ken, who of course had no nautical experience and could hardly be blamed, tried in vain to throw a rope up over the quay – each time it fell short. The same thing happened when Stephen had a go. I looked imploringly towards Doug, far the most practical of us all. Suddenly with a series of acrobatic movements he managed to climb up on the davit and then scramble up on to the harbour wall, taking with him a precious rope. A few moments later, with our feelings somewhat ruffled, especially as quite a few Sunday strollers had been watching us with that inane enjoyment so common to quayside spectators, we had *Sanu* securely tied up to the appropriate bollards.

"Well," said Jess with wifely sarcasm. "What a performance!"

Wisely we didn't prolong the argument, and soon a stroll round the little fishing port revived our spirits. After all we had made our first landfall! Every now and then we turned to look back at

Sanu, her shape looming large and impressive in such a small harbour. By now there were crowds out on a warm Sunday afternoon, but we felt infinitely superior to them all. They had no doubt come in some of the dozens of cars parked in neat rows. We were different—there was our transport, rocking gently by the quay.

By the time we decided to start back the tide had risen and it was just a matter of stepping off the quay on to the deck, and this time unfastening the ropes was child's play. What was not such child's play, I discovered, was extricating *Sanu* from Mevagissey Harbour. She was too big a boat to be turned inside the harbour under power, as she would never come round in the space available (I had not yet learned the trick of using ropes to turn a boat round much more simply). No, the only thing I decided was to reverse out. However, there wasn't all that distance available before the back of the boat might well end up on some nasty looking rocks just beyond the North pier. In the end we solved the problem, somewhat to the amusement of the watchers I fancy, by keeping a forward rope tied on to the bollard and edging the boat backwards—as soon as the bow was clear Stephen freed the rope and jumped aboard, and we were off.

The journey back to Falmouth went smoothly and peacefully. The sun was still shining brightly as we came by St. Anthony and began threading our way up the big channel. This, once again, would be the first time I had brought *Sanu* up to her mooring buoy, and it was not going to be all that easy . . . not only had I to fix the bow dead on to that only buoy, but at the same time I had to make sure I didn't pass too close to the big tugs and other yachts scattered all around. However, with Doug hanging over the side with a boat hook at the ready, I found it not too difficult to bring *Sanu* up in a straight line, at the last moment pulling her fractionally to starboard, and putting the engines furiously into reverse. *Sanu* came to a shuddering standstill: the same moment Doug gave a triumphant shout and hauled up the mooring buoy on his hook. It was then the work of a few minutes to wind in the mooring chain until it was securely fastened on our winch, and we were home and anchored again.

For our next trip, a week later, we decided to go farther afield, and to make a week-end of it all. Fowey was to be our destination this time, that lovely sheltered port much written about by Sir Arthur Quiller-Couch in his romances. Once again I made arduous preliminary investigations. From the Cruising Association's Handbook I learned that the harbour was available at all states of the tide, which was some comfort. However, there was more to be digested, much more. In fact I do not think I can better illustrate the formidable homework awaiting the amateur yachtsman in his tyro stage than be reproducing a few lines from the handbook's well-meant section on Fowey.

"From E. approach with Tr. on Gribben Head, bearing more than 273° to clear the Udder Rock, 3 m. to E. of Fowey, ½ m. off shore, dries 2 ft., rw. cheq can bell buoy. To pass between the Udder and the mainland keep Looe I. shut in by Nealand Point. From S.W., to clear the Cannis Rk. (buoy) a half-tide rock ¼ m. SE from Gribbon Hd, keep Dodman Pt. open to seaward of Gwineas till the tower of Fowey Parish Church, square with 4 pinnacles, comes open of St. Catherine Pt. From SW alternatively to pass between Cannis Rk and the mainland, in 4 ft. LWOS, keep the old castle on Polruan Pt. in line with conspous memorial on Penleath Pt. . . ."

If this reads something like gibberish to you now, remember that at that time it was largely gibberish to me — and it was my job to make use of this information to bring *Sanu* safely into Fowey Harbour. It meant (and of course this was good training) sitting down for a whole evening with a large scale map of Fowey in front of me and painfully identifying each of the places named. I have such a neurosis about the necessity for this preplanning that on paper I should think I have a more thorough knowledge of a whole list of seaports than most people — yet each time we actually came to take *Sanu* anywhere, invariably circumstances seem slightly different from the ones marked out methodically on paper beforehand! Not that I would wish in any way to decry the value of the various sources of information available to amateur navigators. As much as any motorist the boat owner is fed with every possible geographical and topographical factor – short of actually being taken by the wheel and steered into a port, he is given every other help. Then why do things sometimes go curiously wrong? I am afraid there is only one simple answer: the sea is somewhat different to a sheet of paper, and from a ship at sea nothing is ever quite so clear-cut as it seems in a book. Vision may be faulty, distance cannot be accurately judged – above all, landscapes do not somehow identify themselves with the ease they do in a nice clear photograph!

For our trip to Fowey we took a crew mostly of youngsters, between the ages of 11 and 15. This was perhaps a litttle unfortunate for them, as it turned out to be altogether more turbulent than the calm journey to Mevagissey and back. I find recorded in my log: "Lovely sunny day but sea choppy even in Falmouth Harbour. Had lunch sitting in sun on deck while admiring new boats moored around. About 2.30 started engine and set off for Fowey. Very much choppier than we had expected. Easterly wind against us and also tide, and the trip got much rougher around Dodman Point. Peter, Sheila, Jenny all sick, William managed to hold out! Relieved when we reached Gribben Head."

Before we started out Jess reminded me that David Saqui lived at Fowey so it was quite likely *Sanu* would be seeing one of her former owners.

"You'd better not ram the quay this time."

"That just shows," I remarked huffily, "how little you know about these things. There is no quay for a boat of our size – we have to anchor."

This in fact was what was worrying me slightly as, after spying the quite narrow break in the cliffs that marked the entrance to

Fowey, I took *Sanu* slowly up the river. Once on the trip down
with Geoff from Southampton we had anchored, at Salcombe, and
it had been quite a performance handling our huge 160-lb. old
fisherman anchor. Now it was going to be difficult for Doug and
the young boys to heave that monster over the side — for of course I
could not help, being at the wheel. Still, I reassured myself, I had
studied the charts and ascertained that there was a depth of about
eighteen feet where we proposed to anchor, opposite Fowey town.
I knew, too, that you were supposed to play out chain to the length
of three times the depth.

So when I had steered *Sanu* into the proper section of the river
I shouted to Doug to let out the anchor. Manfully he and four of
the boys managed to lift it over the side — and we let out sixty feet
of chain.

"Good," I said, leaning out of the wheel-house window. "That
was very well done. I think . . ." I paused, uneasily. "What is it,
Doug?"

"I was just wondering — do you think we're dragging?"

I looked around nervously.

"We do seem to be moving."

We were, indeed. A few moments later it was alarmingly clear
that our anchor, massive as it was, was not holding, and our boat
was floating cheerfully towards a large yacht which had originally
been some way away. There was nothing for it but to repeat our
original manoeuvre; and in order to do this I had to extricate *Sanu*
from her position, now uncomfortably close to the shore. This
meant reversing — and I had already learned, from our visit to
Mevagissey, that my boat did not steer very well, if at all, in reverse gear. This point was now proved manifestly as I desperately
swung the wheel one way and another. True enough, the reversing
part worked, for in no time at all we had backed straight across
Fowey estuary and were heading (backwards) into the town quay,
where I had time to see quite a few interested spectators gathering.
Supposing, horror of horrors, supposing David Saquie was among

them? If not there now, he jolly well soon would be, called by someone who recognised his former boat.

"For God's sake," I called out. "Let's have another try!"

Giving up the struggle to manoeuvre *Sanu* into a better position, I put her into forward gear again and drove once more towards the opposite bank. At the appropriate time I shouted out to let go the anchor. Doug and the boys, by now covered in sweat and grime, heaved it over again, and . . . after a few agonised moments it became only too clear that we were once again drifting.

"I can't understand it," said Doug shaking his head. "There's sixty feet of chain there. You did say the depth was about eighteen feet, didn't you?"

"Yes."

"Well, there's plenty of chain — and still she's dragging."

I couldn't understand it either; but of course there was a simple enough explanation. In my beginner's over-confidence I had calculated the depth from the chart, forgetting that the figures printed there was for low tide, whereas in fact it was now nearer high tide and (we subsequently discovered) there was a tide difference at Fowey on that day of more than twenty feet. This meant that the depth figure we should have worked on would have been thirty-eight feet, not eighteen — so we should have put out well over 100 feet of chain.

In the heated confusion of those awful moments neither of us stopped to calculate this mistake, of course. Instead, manfully, and in view of a large crowd watching from the town quay, we drove *Sanu* backwards and forwards two more times, each time failing lamentably to settle our anchor. At last, at the point of utter exhaustion, Doug pointed to a coal tanker moored comfortably to a large buoy.

"Let's go alongside her and tie up."

This feat I managed to achieve without any alarming bumps: a couple of seamen on the tanker took our ropes and tied us up — and at long last we were able to shut off our engine.

c*

We flopped around on the deck, most of us either mentally or physically worn out. I looked at the clock. It seemed an eternity since we had so cheerfully entered Fowey estuary – and indeed a whole hour had gone by.

"Ah well," said Doug with a weak smile. "It's all experience."

At that moment a little speedboat came alongside us and someone called out.

"Compliments of David Saqui and he says will you call and see him when you go ashore?"

I groaned.

"My God, he must have been watching."

He had, too, but he kindly made little reference to it when later that evening we sat in his restaurant having coffee and enjoying brushing ourselves up on the earlier history of *Sanu*. Apparently David had carried out the main conversion of the boat, in 1955, and he had subsequently used her for shark trips and also for charting generally.

"That boat, old boy, will go anywhere. Why, to my certain knowledge she's been to every port on the French coast from Boulogne down to Brest. And the Dutch canals, too. Oh, you've got a good boat there, I can tell you."

David showed us some coloured photographs of *Sanu* in her early days, with the hull painted a delicate light blue – she really looked superb, for a boat of her size and shape.

By the time, late that night, we came out and climbed into our dinghy to run over to *Sanu* we had recovered from our sense of humiliation. It was a lovely starlit night, there was a moon hovering on the horizon, and Fowey harbour glistened and glittered like a fairyland. This was the life! We chugged out to *Sanu* and climbed up the ladder, and stood on deck for a while looking around at the quite magical scene. It was, after all, our first night away on a trip on our own account, and we could but feel a sense of excitement, if only to contemplate all the other nights to come.

In the morning, too, this sense of excitement prevailed. It was a

Sunday and the Fowey Yacht Club boats were out racing about the wide river mouth, and using our boat, I fancy, as a turning point. We sat on deck watching all this unfamiliar activity, while Stephen and his pals took the dinghy and went for a long exploration up river, past the huge china clay tankers which lay like lurking monsters behind wooded banks. During the morning David came out in a friend's boat and had a quick look round his former charge, showing us where changes had been made. Later we waved goodbye and watched him pass on to the open hull of a boat which he had recently purchased for making another conversion.

After lunch we untied *Sanu* from her mooring buoy (the tanker had slipped off during the night leaving us in comfortable possession) and headed out to sea again. I am glad to say we made quite a professional departure! Conditions at sea had quietened down a bit; there was still a bad swell but nothing serious, and we bowled along at our steady seven knots enjoying the exhilaration of wind and sun. As usual I was somewhat chained to the wheel, but I had the window down and enjoyed staring about me. Sometimes Doug would stand up at the bow keeping an eye out for strange fish or boats. It was always interesting on those coastal trips, for you never knew what would come next!

For us, it took the form of an unexpected rescue operation. We were nearing Falmouth, about opposite Portmellon Head, and I was just beginning to head for St. Anthony, when Doug gave a shout.

"There's someone waving to us, over there."

We all lined the side and stared, and sure enough over near the shore was a small boat with someone standing up and waving a white handkerchief or sheet.

We agreed that we had better investigate, so I brought *Sanu* round and headed towards the shore, then turned away and held her steady. By now we saw that it was a motor speed-boat, presumably broken down, and a man had been rowing desperately —

but, unfortunately for him, against the tide. In fact they were being carried steadily away from Falmouth, down the coast.

Now they managed to come alongside. We put down the ladder and helped the three occupants aboard, then tied their boat on at our stern.

"Don't worry," I said. "We'll soon have you back in Falmouth."

Having spent hours myself studying nautical books about the subject of salvage I was rather amused to find our three passengers behaving rather oddly – hardly speaking, keeping very quiet, and obviously just waiting till they could get away from us. I found this understandable, for the secret terror of anyone who breaks down at sea is the risk of having to pay salvage. I do not know whether we would have been entitled to claim salvage, quite possibly we would, but in the circumstances it would have seemed rather mean and naturally we were glad to give a helping hand. All the same, we hardly picked up our anchor at Falmouth when our three passengers were on their boat and off!

Our final week-end trip along the South Coast was to be our most ambitious – a visit to the home of Sir Francis Drake and his merry men, the port of Plymouth. This was one case, I discovered, where the sea route was much shorter than the road, for by car from Falmouth to Plymouth must be eighty miles, whereas studying our charts we now found that the direct sea passage would be about half that. Not, of course, that it would save any time; at our rate of just over seven knots we would take well over five hours. Furthermore another look at the chart showed that the direct route from Falmouth in a straight line to Rame Head would mean spending several hours well out at sea, possibly out of sight of land.

Not surprisingly the prospect of navigating *Sanu* into the heart of busy Plymouth Sound filled me with some misgivings, these were hardly allayed by reading the extensive warnings and cautions in the relevant pages of the guides. "Keep a good lookout for submarines," warned the *Cruising Association Handbook*, which went on to list no fewer than ten possible anchorages, all sounding strangely complicated to a novice. Some of these involved anchoring, a process which hardly appealed to me after our experience at Fowey, and so I decided to try for mooring at a quay. There seemed to be several possibilities and I made quite a few phone calls before finally finding that the Royal Western Yacht Club of England was responsible for a line of moorings in Millbay Dock, one of which I could have.

By the time we set off from Falmouth soon after two o'clock I had been over my passage, on paper, night after night during the preceding week, and felt I had everything worked out pretty well. But of course as soon as we had left the familiarity of Dodman Point and headed on a course of about 260° for distant and unseen Rame Head, some twenty-odd miles away, I began to grow nervous at the prospect of losing touch with land. Playing safe — which further experience has taught me is never a bad thing at sea — I kept close enough to the land to be able to recognise landmarks like Gribben Head, by Fowey, and later Looe Island — with the result that we did our trip to Rame Head in the form of a slight curve, covering more ground than was necessary, but feeling less worried than if we had been out in the ocean blue.

Once we spied Rame Head then I was able to head *Sanu* confidently to seaward and then bring her round into Plymouth Sound past Penlee Point and towards the breakwater. Now we had to follow a pattern of buoys that would take us down past Drake's Island. I must admit that although in one sense it was exhilarating to be in the centre of the Sound, and spy the famous Hoe and its surrounding Georgian buildings ahead, I was more relieved when at last we spied the entrance to Millbay Dock. Just as we steamed past the pierhead and prepared to look for the mooring we had been told about, a man with a megaphone hailed us at close quarters and called out that as it was a week-end, and there was no traffic, we could moor at the main pier.

Millbay Dock proved quite an impressive experience. The fact was, we discovered, the Plymouth authorities had decided to cater for yachtsmen in an imaginative way : a long row of double moorings had been laid out some way from the quay where we tied up – in addition there was an inner yacht basin, whose gates were opened for an hour or two at every high tide, and there you could lay your yacht up as long as you liked. There was a charge of 10s. per night, but as this covered your whole boat's contingent, and also entitled one to hot and cold showers and the use of a changing room, etc., it seemed pretty good value.

Millbay Dock was, of course, also a commercial dock, and though quiet on a week-end, full of interest for the children. In fact we were followed in by a huge modern tanker flying an unfamiliar foreign flag, and we watched with fascination as she was edged into her berth across the water, by a system of tugs and ropes. Soon after Stephen and his friend Nicky and the other children piled into the dinghy and set off on a tour of the dock. Not altogether by chance, I feel, they pulled alongside the modern tanker and to their delight were invited aboard and treated to a first-hand tour of inspection of what turned out to be a brand new Rumanian ship which, according to the children, was beautifully fitted up, even having its own cinema. One wonders how many British freighter firms cater for their crew in quite this style.

Altogether we enjoyed our visit to Plymouth much more than we anticipated. Our berth was only a few minutes walk from Plymouth Hoe below which stretched a series of marvellous open-air swimming pools built into the rocks. All around was a majestic vista of the Sound as seen from the land – soon we would be seeing it from a different angle, we reflected with the smugness of boat owners.

When it came to leaving on the Sunday afternoon we were somewhat rattled to be told by a passing naval officer that there were gales in the English Channel, and we feared the worst. However, once round Rame Head we encountered nothing worse than Force 3–4, slackening off, and in fact our worrying experience was not roughness, but mist. At first we hardly realised it was coming upon us, but soon I had to admit uneasily that we could no longer see the coastline. For some time I held on to a course which would theoretically bring us to Dodman Point, but in the end the swirling clouds alarmed me so much that I felt I simply must see some of the coastline to estimate where we were. My big worry, of course, was that we might go wrong on our course and carry too far out to sea, in which case we might not only miss Dodman Point, but also Falmouth and perhaps even the Lizard. That at least was my justification for heading *Sanu* considerably off course to starboard, so that she should come nearer to the coast. I realise now that this was possibly rather a risky thing to do; but as it happened it achieved its rather dismal result — suddenly there was a break in the mist and we spied tall cliffs which proved to be around Fowey! This meant we had not travelled as far as I had hoped, and we then had to reset our course and head up towards Dodman Point. The mist was still thick, and on top of that we had to take a big swell on our beam so that *Sanu* began heeling over quite alarmingly. At such times everyone might be thrown all over the place and it was very worrying if one of the children was not to be seen, so that Doug was constantly occupied pacing round and checking up on everyone's safety. I for my part was glued to the wheel trying to devise a method of heading *Sanu* into each wave so that she did not heel over too disturbingly. This time no one was actually sick, but all a little frightened, and very tired. The last hour seemed to take an eternity, and it was nearly eight o'clock in the evening and approaching dusk when finally we sighted the familiar St. Anthony lighthouse and headed for our mooring buoy. It had been a long and rather tiring week-end, but I felt in my heart it had been excellent experience. Very gradually *Sanu*'s operators were beginning to acquire a certain touch of professionalism. . . . Time now for sailing farther afield.

6

The Home-coming

EVER since we were able to acquire a boat of our own we had naturally looked forward one day to sailing her proudly into our own home port, St. Ives. Among other things it was exasperating to be living in a house on the edge of the sea and yet have to travel twenty-five miles to go aboard our boat. We realised that it would not be wise or comfortable to keep *Sanu* permanently at St. Ives, but there was no reason at all why we should not moor there from time to time, and the summer months would obviously be the most suitable.

I can remember when Jess and I decided it was time to make the trip. It was one of those utterly calm summer evenings when nothing stirred. We had climbed on top of the Island and from there we looked across the inner part of the bay – and there, in a beautiful cluster of blue and green and white and red, were about ten of the French crabbers that came over regularly from Audierne, in Brittany. Across the bay the late sunshine illuminated the whole scene with a poignant beauty: in the background the long line of Hayle sands, nearer the sea-green mirror of sea and the brightness of the crabbers, and nearer still the beautiful gold spread of St. Ives's own beaches. Just behind the rooftops we could glimpse the bustle of smaller boats in the harbour itself. . . . Altogether it was a fairylike spectacle.

"Just imagine," I squeezed Jess's hand romantically, "sailing round in *Sanu*, maybe dropping anchor for a while out by the French boats – then the kids could enjoy going ashore in the dinghy and bringing all their friends aboard. Oh, won't they enjoy themselves!"

We spent quite a while standing on top of the Island looking down on the French crabbers lying still and almost immovable in the calm sea. Long after we had walked on I kept remembering that view, only in my mind it was *Sanu*'s familiar shape that lay there so placidly at anchor. . . . If only I could have guessed at the future!

For our trip round from Falmouth we persuaded our great friends Anthony and Christianne to come along, with their son Paul. We decided to make a long week-end of it and drove over to Falmouth on the Friday evening, so that we were able to enjoy an evening at the King's Head and a night's sleep in Falmouth Harbour before preparing the next morning for the first part of the trip, the voyage from Falmouth round the Lizard and across Mount's Bay to Newlyn.

Perhaps because of the experience of several previous trips I found this one much more relaxed than in the past. It was, anyway, a lovely day, and the sea was calm except for the inevitable slow swell. Everyone lay sunbathing on the deck except the poor old skipper, but even I got my ration by leaning out of the open window.

Not long after passing Black Rock and heading towards the Lizard, Doug and Stephen, standing up front, gave excited shouts and pointed.

"Sharks! Basking sharks! Dozens of them!"

Fascinated, we crossed to the side and watched the long dark fins rising up out of the depths. Basking sharks are a common enough sight in Cornish coastal waters, but it was the first time we had seen any. They didn't seem at all interested in us, and soon we had left them behind.

Now that we were closing in on the Lizard I realised why it

is treated with such respect by mariners. All around, for some distance from its base, stretched rows of jagged and fearsome looking rocks, some awash, some recognisable only by the white swirl of disturbed foam above. We had been warned that once out of shelter of the land one might well encounter some wind on rounding the Lizard, but on this day all was quiet, even the inevitable race, which is to be found around most points, was mild by comparison with the one at Portland we had traversed earlier in the year.

Soon we had rounded the point with its formidable line of cliffs and, nestling on top, that large black and white lighthouse familiar to navigators from all over the world for whom, in many cases, it is the first glimpse of England. Now I altered course considerably to bring *Sanu* on to a line of about 320° to bring us across Mount's Bay towards Newlyn and Penzance. The journey from Falmouth to Lizard had taken us nearly two hours and now it was to be another two hours before we reached Newlyn – however, we were travelling past very familiar country, and had little difficulty in spying Looe Bar, the fishing port of Porthleven and then the long white line of Prah Sands. Next, looming mysteriously out of the water, we saw the fabulous St. Michael's Mount, which looked rather grimmer from the sea than from land.

By now the water was so calm that it was almost glassy, with a strange velvety composure – it was so absolutely perfect and still that somehow, almost by instinct, I felt uneasy. Surely this was too good to be true? Still, for the moment it was true, and in these idyllic calm conditions I headed *Sanu* across what is locally known as Gwavas Lake and towards the narrow entrance to Newlyn Harbour. Here my experience at Mevagissey was useful and I managed to bring the boat in at a fairly oblique angle, thus avoiding the necessity for too sharp a turn, and we came round towards the long north quay where, much to my relief, I spied a long stretch of quay wall that was deserted of craft. Actually this was most unusual for Newlyn where boats are invariably moored in lines of three or four at a time, but we were fortunate as several big boats were still out fishing.

After tying up securely we settled down to one of those welcome hot meals which Jess had got in the habit of setting in motion even while still at sea. When it was served around the saloon table there were in all thirteen of us squashed merrily together, a bit cramped really, but all very friendly — and were we hungry! Christianne and Anthony had thoroughly enjoyed the experience, and we spent much of the evening down at the old Tolcarne Inn at Newlyn (which was flooded out in the disastrous Penzance floods of a year previously) planning all kinds of future trips.

Alas, the next morning, that velvety glassy look had proved a false one and conditions had changed ominously. When I walked with Martin to get some Sunday papers a cutting wind bit at our legs and buffeted us about. What would it be like out at sea?

For some time I could not make up my mind what to do. It was all very awkward, for several more friends had come over from St. Ives to enjoy a Sunday trip round, and I hated to disappoint them. Among them, too, was a St. Ives fisherman, William, who had promised to show us the quickest and safest way round Land's End, so we were well prepared. All the same. . . .

In the end I fell back on my favourite safeguard, and went and rang up the St. Ives lifeguards. When I gathered from them that there was a freshening north-north-west wind blowing up, and already Force 5, then I knew in my heart that caution must be the maxim. After all, I worked out, there would be seventeen people aboard the ship, and I would never forgive myself if I took them out and anything happened. It wasn't as if we *had* to get to St. Ives; our boating was supposed to be for pleasure.

So we spent the day in Newlyn Harbour making the best of things and then, inevitable anticlimax, made our way back by bus and taxi to St. Ives. However, when we came over the hill and I saw the state of the sea, I was thankful that I had made the decision I did.

During that week I managed most afternoons to get over to Newlyn and work on the boat, sorting and tidying up. I found it interesting to be in the working centre of a big commercial fishing port like Newlyn — the atmosphere was subtly different from ports like St. Ives, where pleasure-boating has become all-important. The fishermen worked hard long hours, often at sea for several days — sometimes travelling 200 miles: in return they earned good money. Catches of up to 1,000 stone from one trip were not infrequent, and wages sometimes reached £50 per week. Newlyn was a very busy place.

For this very reason, of course, *Sanu* was not altogether a popular visitor, especially as after a day or two several big long liners came in. Almost every day I found the boat in a different position, one day against the wall, another moved to the outside to accommodate a boat with a catch to unload. In general the fishermen were very good about this, but some of the Belgian and French trawlers that came in were inclined to be somewhat casual about bumping bows and sterns, and I did not need a tip from the harbour's staff to realise that the sooner we moved out the better.

All the same I enjoyed the week in Newlyn where, among the special pleasures, was the presence of a sister of *Sanu*, the working M.F.V. *Karenza*, which was one of the batch of fifty such craft built by Curtis's of Looe in 1942. She was, of course, laid out inside different to *Sanu*, being used entirely for fishing, but there was the same old Kelvin 88. Skipper Billy Love had just repainted *Karenza* and she was a treat to behold — reminding Jess and I that we had quite a lot to do to *Sanu*, much of which would now have to wait till the winter.

At the end of the week we prepared once more to bring *Sanu* round to St. Ives. Still possessed by my romantic memory of the French crabbers moored in the bay I thought it would be rather nice to arrive in the late evening and anchor for the night. I had visions of a full moon riding over the bay and some of us sitting on deck in the warm evening looking languidly over at the lights of our own homes in St. Ives.

This time Anthony and Christianne were unable to get away, but several people came on the spur of the moment, including Michael Black, a sculptor we knew, Jack, a potter at the Leach Pottery, two friends of Doug's, Pat and David.

From Newlyn down the south coast as far as the Runnelstone was a pleasant trip, travelling quite close to the land and recognising familiar spots like Lamorna Cove and Penberth, and the Minack Theatre at Porthcurno. The cliffs along this stretch have a haunting, rather grim beauty of their own – it is magnificent to behold but any seaman will feel uneasy, remembering countless tales of boats being dashed to pieces upon those beautiful stones. Indeed, only a few weeks previously a French crabber had gone aground in fog and the crew lost.

So, as we rounded the Runnelstone and now came up to the famous Longship Lighthouse at Land's End, my fascination with the scenery remained tempered with a certain nervousness. I must admit it was an exhilarating experience seeing this familiar edifice from such an unfamiliar angle – and, yes, over there were the same sands at Sennen Cove along which I used to walk staring wistfully out to sea! We were temporarily on one of the busy shipping lanes, and looking around I counted no fewer than six other boats in sight, one or two quite large tankers, the rest smaller cargo boats bound for Wales or coming round perhaps to Falmouth. We also passed one of the Newlyn trawlers stationary, pulling in nets, and exchanged waves. Everything seemed rather timeless and romantic.

Alas, after rounding the Longships and passing close to the formidable Brisons and Cape Cornwall (England's only cape), things began to change – for the worse. All at once we found ourselves taking a huge swell on our beam: with every wave *Sanu* was lifted up and turned half-way round and then down with a sinking feeling. By the time we had reached Penlee Lighthouse, still some ten miles from St. Ives, we knew we were in for a really rough passage. Owing to the fact we had made a rather late start, too, instead of having the tide with us it had turned, so that progress up the north coast became excruciatingly slow.

One by one our last-minute guests began to look pale, and then green: finally sickness became a general order. Everyone, including ourselves, felt more and more miserable. I had got conditioned to the sea by now, as had Doug, but both of us stared out of the wheel-house window at the passing coast willing it to move more quickly past us. It seemed that we would never reach St. Ives: to pass Gurnard's Head seemed to take about half an hour, the same for Zennor Point.

At last, struggling all the time, *Sanu* broke round the corner and suddenly we had a strange new view of our own Porthmeor Beach — from the sea. As a matter of fact, it was rather an alarming view, for huge white breakers were rolling up the sands and licking at the foot of our doorway, so we would have known that it was a bad sea if we had been on land. Alas, we *were* out at sea, and it was a bad one!

When finally we rounded the Island and came in sight of that patch of the bay where the French crabbers had lain so peacefully at anchor — there were not ten of them, but one solitary boat. And that was tossing about wildly in the rough sea.

I looked at Jess in dismay.

"Not exactly as planned!"

Far from it, indeed. It was near low tide so we couldn't have changed our minds and gone into St. Ives Harbour even if we had wanted to. And, anyway, I wouldn't have fancied it, for after we had come round near to the French crabber and put out our anchor we saw that the waves were coming in at a great pace right across the entrance to the harbour. It would have been a difficult job to handle even a large boat like *Sanu* without danger of her being carried against the harbour wall. As for the dinghy . . .

"No." I shook my head firmly. "It would be absolutely mad to try to get ashore in the dinghy now."

Michael Black, who had a phone call to make at 11 p.m. was indignant.

"Oh, but surely—"

Half-heartedly we made an effort to lower the dinghy. It was immediately tossed up higher than the boat, and then plunged down again. Quickly we hauled it in.

"I'm very sorry," I said as firmly as I could manage for a captain who, though he knew his word was law, was feeling pretty miserable about the whole affair. "We just can't risk taking the dinghy ashore in these conditions. We'll spend the night aboard, and then in the morning perhaps things will be better."

I shall never forget that night. To begin with, only recently I had decided to dispense with our original huge fisherman anchor, weighing 160 lb. and needing three or four people to handle it. In its place I had bought a 100 lb. C.Q.R. anchor, which is sometimes known as the plough anchor, which I knew to be much more effective than a fisherman, and also could be handled by two people. Now that we had to use this anchor for the first time under somewhat trying circumstances I could not help being worried. Supposing it proved a failure? Supposing it dragged? What if we ended up on the rocks of our own home port? Disastrous—utter humiliation!

It was half-past ten at night by now, and the occupants of *Sanu* remained in a rather sad and sorry state, particularly as reaching St. Ives had brought no real respite. Whatever those French crabbers may have looked like on that faraway mythical summer evening, the reality of now was totally different. A big wind was blowing in from the north; each swell picked up *Sanu*, tossed her one way and then another, deposited her for an illusory moment in absolute stillness—then picked her up again and started the whole revolting process again. Naturally being at anchor we were quite helpless to take any avoiding action. We could see the bright

lights of St. Ives only 200 yards away, but they might as well have been 200 miles away for all the use they were to us. They served only as a tantalising reminder of what might have been. Jess and I played with rosy fantasies of being at home sitting comfortably in a comfortable couch, relaxing, without any worries. . . .

Whereas in fact we were stuck on *Sanu* for the whole of the night. And what a night! After a while the others tried to bed themselves down in various conditions of misery, some in the aft cabin, others scattered about not much caring where. For Doug and I, sleep was impossible, and we settled ourselves down in the wheel-house to keep uneasy watch on the all-prevailing problem — was *Sanu* staying where she was? We used two main guides — first, the bright lights of the Porthminster Hotel, almost directly opposite us. Every few minutes I stared fixedly at those yellow winks, estimating purposefully if they were still at the same distance. The other guide was a small mooring buoy which Doug had noticed as we came in to drop our anchor, and which lay a few yards from our bow. This buoy was to do much to sustain our spirits, for every time, fearfully, one of us walked out on the deck to check its position he came back smiling smugly and saying: "No, it's not moved, so we can't be dragging." Only much later the next morning, when we prepared to move, did we make the discovery that our anchor had become entangled with that buoy and that of course it hadn't shifted, relatively – it had been firmly attached to us!

We had a third possible bearing in the nearby shape and lights of the solitary French crabber, but this was almost more worry than it was worth, for sometimes, shifting in the tides, we seemed to blow dangerously near to one another. When, half-way through the night, another French trawler came and moored quite close, that gave us yet another headache.

We were quite surprised, really, at the night's activity. About one o'clock we saw a searchlight cutting across the water and recognised the new St. Ives fishing boat, *Rose of Sharon*, a Scot-built boat with 120-h.p. Gardner engines whose speed was re-putedly ten knots. She was coming back from a fishing trip and as it was now high tide was obviously going to go into harbour, de-spite the rough sea. We watched full of admiration as her skipper took her straight in across the big waves – an admiration that in-creased when after a few moments she came out again and disap-peared into the darkness over towards Hayle Estuary. On such a night, they must have decided, Hayle would be rather more com-fortable than in St. Ives Harbour. Or the bay!

During the night one or two more local fishing boats loomed out of the darkness and either anchored or went in – naturally with their local knowledge this feat was safe enough, but I did not fancy making my first entry into the harbour in pitch blackness. No, we would wait till the daylight and then see how things were.

Alas, sea-wise, they were not a great deal better. The waves were still pounding in, and everything was grey and uninviting. About ten o'clock, however, the sea quietened down a little, and just then a large motor launch came out bearing our friend Anthony and one or two others, and also bringing a message: "Were we intending to put into Hayle, and if so did we want the services of a pilot?"

In preparation for possibly going into Hayle I had made extensive study of the entry there. Across the estuary there is a sand bar which cannot be crossed at low tide. Even at higher states of the tide, when entry is possible, the channel is a narrow and difficult one. Only recently a Dutch cargo boat had landed up on Hayle Sands and been stuck there for days before she could be pulled off by tugs. On paper I felt I knew how to take *Sanu* into Hayle, especially on a fine calm day. But this was not quite those sort of conditions. . . .

"Go on," said Jess, "have a pilot this time at least. Then you'll feel safe."

So we had one of the St. Ives pilots, and were very glad of his services, for in fact the sea was quite heavy over at Hayle, and we had the quite uncanny experience of literally "surfing" into the narrow channel. I would have been petrified, but the pilot appeared quite unruffled giving a running commentary as we approached about how we should fix two beacons in line and steer for them with Lelant Church just behind. In his wish to be helpful he went out of his way to tell us just when we were a few feet over the bar, also jovially pointing out swirls of white froth which indicated patches where we would have gone aground. One way and another there were, indeed, some breathless moments before finally we passed over the bar and crept slowly up to our destination, Lelant Quay, near the ferry crossing and golf course. The approach to this was a channel only a few feet wider than *Sanu*, but this held no worries for our pilot, and with consummate ease he brought our boat up to the Quay where we soon got ropes ashore.

No sooner had we thanked the pilot and paid the regulation fee of £2 10s., which in the circumstances was obviously money well spent, than he was off again in a waiting motor-boat to go out to sea and pilot in one of the tankers lying around waiting to come into Hayle and unload. In fact this stretch of north coast of Cornwall is so bereft of sheltered harbours that Hayle remains quite a busy seaport. We had often watched in fascination from Lelant as quite large ships came gliding up – towering high above our puny figures, standing at the water's edge. Of course, bringing a 300-ton tanker into Hayle was a considerably trickier job altogether than bringing in a 60-ft. M.F.V., but now we felt a sense of real comradeship.

And so, at two o'clock in the afternoon, nearly twenty-four hours after leaving Newlyn, we were at last on dry land again. It was unbelievable, too good to be true. We stamped about the long quay, tying up ropes and basking in the sheer delight of being able to walk on solid land again. Then:

"Hey, isn't there something you've forgotten?"

It was Doug, reminding us that for the first time we were going to have to use one of our massive wooden legs, the port one, to stop *Sanu* from tipping over when the tide went out. The next quarter of an hour was not a happy one. We were tired and irritable, we had never handled the leg before, and the whole business proved far more complicated than we had imagined. It was just as well we had a large crew! Four people had to handle the leg, while Doug went down into the engine room to manoeuvre the long bolt through the prepared hole. Juggling with a dead weight and getting it into exactly the right position in line with a hole and a bolt was hardly the occupation for tired mariners. However, at last the deed was accomplished and *Sanu* safely tucked away, and we could go home – ignominiously, somehow, by bus!

After all that, we reflected the next day, we had still not made our official entry into St. Ives, triumphal or otherwise. By an ironic chance another, smaller M.F.V. had called into the harbour later on the day we had gone to Hayle, and quite a few of our friends, having heard of our impending arrival, assumed that was our boat. So, one way and another, it really was time we made a flesh and blood appearance.

Whenever Jess had a nightmare, in those days, it was that I would bring *Sanu* into St. Ives as I brought her into Mevagissey — that is, hitting the harbour wall with a resounding clump. I must say it was a fear which I shared, too, though my greatest apprehension of all was always that the boat's engine would stop at some vitally important moment. Still I could understand Jess's dread; and so when finally a few of us went to Hayle to bring *Sanu* over to St. Ives, I was determined not to let the family honour down. We made a rather bad beginning, in that for half an hour we could not get the Kelvin engine to work, one of the few occasions it has ever been difficult. As I had timed our exit from Hayle around high tide and now it was already past I began to get worried, but fortunately at last she caught, and I rushed up to the wheel-house and began directing Stephen and his friend to untie the ropes. There was a tricky moment or two turning the boat round in the narrow estuary, then we were off towards the sea, travelling quite fast, for now we had the tide with us.

I found it quite easy to steer *Sanu* out parallel to the guiding posts, and soon we were across the bay and heading for the north quay at St. Ives. Several of our friends who had heard of our plan were down on the quay waiting to cheer us in, and I suppose the word spread for there seemed quite a cluster of people, including the harbour master, Dickie Admiral.

"Ahem!" said Jess with foreboding.

"It's all right," I said, panting as I swung the wheel round and back and round and back, edging the boat in towards the wall. "I — won't hit-the-wall."

Neither, I'm glad to say, did we. In fact we made an entry which I heard described later by a fisherman as "proper professional". (Mind you that was just once — on a later occasion, unexpectedly finding the fishery protection vessel H.M.S. *Squirrel* moored in my intended berth, I had to swerve out and come in again, and did in fact give *Sanu* a nasty bash.) Stephen and his friends jumped ashore with the ropes, and soon we were securely tied up and welcoming the harbour master aboard for a drink to mark the occasion.

"Are you sure we'll be all right here?" I asked anxiously, for the last thing I wanted to do was to fall out with the local fishermen.

"Yes, yes, cap'n, you're alright here for the while. And later on, if you're staying we can move you up the quay."

This in fact was what we did during the odd weeks we spent in St. Ives. When we first came in we moored wherever there was a convenient space; then, the next day, perhaps, pulled the boat farther up by rope, to get her out of the way of where the larger boats landed their catches.

The period that now ensured was one of forgivable smugness. After all *Sanu* was our boat, and here she lay respondent and shining in St. Ives, for all to see. We were proud of her, too, and delighted in showing her off to our friends. None of them, I fancy, had quite realised what a big boat she was but, of course, we are a big family, and need a boat of this size. The accommodation amazed everyone, but in the long run it was the boat itself, her obvious strength and stability and seaworthiness, that made the biggest impression. I was often amused to hear some of the less favourably disposed of the fishermen struggling to phrase what they wanted to say — which was on the lines of: "I don't approve of the Val Bakers, those amateur seamen, but I must admit they've got a good boat there." That, of course, was the unavoidable truth about *Sanu*. She was not only a good boat, she was in fact just the very kind of boat that fishermen liked to see around. To this day I have never heard anyone speak ill of her as a sea boat.

From the beginning the harbour master was very kind to us and did his best to make things as normal as possible, but of course our very size proved something of a handicap. As far as the few large fishing boats were concerned they wished us elsewhere as there always existed the possibility that we occupied space they needed at the quay side – while so far as the small boats were concerned they lived, I think, in secret terror that we would somehow cause them some damage. I could sympathise with both points of view, and yet I could not really agree. A harbour is surely meant for common use, and we should all be able to manage together, working boats and pleasure boats.

Still, apart from a few inevitable pin-pricks we were very happy to be moored at St. Ives – and for our children, of course, it was a halcyon period. Day after day they had their friends down and showed them over the boat, or used *Sanu* as a base for bathing when the tide was up. This was the time when our aft cabin came into its own as a sort of club centre. Stephen and his boy friends, Demelza and her girl friends, Genevieve and her younger group of friends, all somehow piled in. And if they weren't there, or bathing, then they would be out rowing in the pram, or persuading Stephen to take them for a run in the motor dinghy.

Meantime Jess and I took advantage of this first opportunity to see *Sanu* in the round, so to speak. At St. Ives the harbour dries out, and twice a day *Sanu* was dry, leaning against the quay with a leg out on the other side. We were pleasantly surprised by what we saw, in some fearfulness, we walked across the sands and stood under the towering hull. Apart from a few barnacles it seemed in excellent condition – and we soon got Stephen and his friends on the job of clearing away the barnacles.

It has been my experience that, as with friends, so with a boat there is no end to the discoveries to be made – and with every experience relationship deepens or collapses. It was so now with *Sanu*. Somehow, being able to see her thus exposed, to stand parallel with the enormous propeller and look at strange bolts and valves and other half-hidden attributes normally hidden below the water line – made us much more aware of her as a character.

Among other things we got a truer feeling of her size — she really was VAST, seen out of the water. Indeed she was the biggest of all the St. Ives boats to be seen! And she was ours.

"Ah, you've a good boat there," said Dicky Admiral, the harbour master. "Take you anywhere — anywhere in the world."

7

Crossing the Channel

DURING that glorious summer in St. Ives we had often imagined making a really long trip in *Sanu*. It was almost a drawback of owning a boat so large and ambitious that the mere idea of taking her out for a quiet spin round the bay seemed rather ludicrous! No, a boat like *Sanu* demanded something altogether more ambitious and adventurous. To the Mediterranean! To the Greek Isles! To the South Seas!

Well, we weren't quite up to that sort of trip as yet: but with the experience of our various coastal trips behind us we did feel capable of venturing farther afloat. Besides, the summer was getting on, and it would be a nice climax to embark on a really memorable journey, not for just a week-end or a few days, but for several weeks. Now that the school summer holidays were approaching the children would be free, and though the early part of August would confine us to St. Ives because of our pottery business, it should be possible to manage a holiday at the beginning of September.

I began studying maps and charts and contemplating the various possibilities. Ireland lay only about 130 miles away and sounded an exciting trip; the west coast seemed to have dozens of attractive anchorages. Or what about a trip up the Welsh coast and perhaps on to Scotland? I had always dreamed of meandering about the Western Isles in my own boat. Or we could emulate the French fishermen whose boats so often lay anchored in St. Ives Bay, and make the reverse journey across to Brest and Audierne, and

D

wander down the coast of Britanny. . . . Mind you, come to think of it, it was supposed to be a pretty dangerous area, exposed to the Atlantic as it was. And then there might be some language difficulty, a different system of navigation and so forth?

In the end we evolved a compromise — somewhere far enough to represent a major voyage, quite foreign-seeming in many ways, yet still an English-speaking area — and at the same time, somewhere very beautiful and full of variety, as well as offering special scope for the amateur yachtsman. I refer, of course, to the Channel Islands. More than twenty years ago I had visited Guernsey and Jersey very briefly and felt pleasantly attracted: islands, anyway, have always had a fascination for me. Now it would surely be delightful to meander between the islands in our very own boat, mooring a night here, a night there.

We began to plan. Goodness me, how we planned! We might have been setting off for the South Seas to judge by the amount of preparations that went on — and yet, when one paused to consider the matter, there wasn't much that could have been skimped. We expected to be away about seventeen days, and for that period *Sanu* would be completely our home. This meant, on the domestic front alone, stocking up with plenty of tinned and packeted food to supplement the fresh foods we would hope to pick up day by day. Blankets and sheets, Calor gas, fuel oil, water — little wonder that for the last week before setting off we spent most of the time running backwards and forwards from our house down to *Sanu*, moored for the time being in St. Ives Harbour.

For me the excitement took a different and sometimes apprehensive form. On many of our previous trips I had been able to rely on the very practical help of Doug Rowe, and the knowledge of his experience of diesel engines in case anything should go wrong. Now he was involved in his skin-diving expedition on the Scillies and would be unable to make our long trip to the Channel Islands. In any case I felt that it would be a good thing for me to have to stand on my own ship, so to speak. With experience I had come to understand quite a lot about our Kelvin engine, and so had my son, Stephen, who fortunately had a scientific turn of mind. I had learned the knack of starting the engine on the handle with no more than a half turn, and stamped into my memory now were the various processes necessary. On a short trip to Newquay and back I had managed engine and boat quite reasonably: so now for it.

It was my job, as skipper and navigator, to prepare thoroughly for the voyage, from beginning to end. Long before we ever left St. Ives Harbour I had travelled in *Sanu* dozens of times along the English coast and over the Channel and round those scattered little islands. I did this, of course, sitting tucked away in my office with every inch of space covered with charts and books of reference. Altogether I bought about a dozen large-scale Admiralty Charts, covering the Western Section of the English Channel; the west, central and eastern portions of Guernsey; Herm and Sark; the West, central and eastern portions of Jersey; and Alderney, general, and Alderney Harbour. I also obtained a couple of other maps covering the areas down by St. Malo, in Brittany — just in case! In addition, and this really was like a Bible to me, I bought that invaluable book by K. Adlard Coles, *Channel Harbours and Anchorages*, with its detailed section on the Channel Islands. Like every other amateur yachtsman, I fancy, I had the delightful feeling that the book had been written especially for me, for somehow Adlard Coles seemed to understand just the sort of information that I would require even down to tiny little diagrams to illustrate the look of a beacon or other mark. The photographs were also wonderfully helpful, showing just the view of a harbour entrance you would want.

In some ways, however, I found the book somewhat disturbing!

"The scene in the Channel Island at high water is one of islands with a few outlying rocks, towers and tops of beacons standing out of the water: but at low water the rocks will have grown to islets, the beacons will be on top of rocks as big as houses, and vast

areas of islets, rocks, ledges and sands will be uncovered. A small
isolated rock is known locally as a "boue" and much can be done
to avoid these dangers by keeping a watch for them, as our fore-
fathers used to do before the era of aids to navigation. In a smooth
sea rocks below the surface can sometimes be seen, and if there is a
strong tide they will be revealed by ripples and circles of oily looking water. If it is a little rough there will be overfalls over the
rocks, and if a swell is running the waves will break, spurting
white columns of spray. It will be seen on the chart that some of
the larger rocks which are always above water are steep-to. Such
rocks can be treated like light-houses. By passing close to them the
yacht's position can be fixed, and in thick weather one can sometimes make short hops from one rock to another, rather than losing
one's position in open water, where there may be isolated rocks.
Rocks with the sea crashing over them may be quite awe inspiring,
but in reality they are friends, and the enemies are those which lie
beneath the surface."

There was much more in the same vein. Although I found some
small comfort in Adlard Coles's concluding words, "All that is
required in the Channel Islands is an extra degree of caution and
vigilance", I must admit that the more intensively I planned and
studied our trip, the more I began to wish we were bound for
almost anywhere else.

For a trip of this kind we naturally hoped to take some friends
along, and were delighted when a fellow writer, Frank Baker, his
wife, Katie, and their teenage daughter, Josephine, said they
could come. Although not in any way related, despite our name,
Frank and I had discovered a good deal in common, notably a
great love of Cornwall and the long and traumatic experience of
raising a large family. As a result we shared a sense of humour,
which I fancied on such a trip we might well need. Jess and I were
touched by the enthusiasm and gaiety with which Frank and Katie
looked forward to the trip, for one or two other friends had disappointed us by their obvious unwillingness to come on any of our

voyages. After all, we *had* prepared ourselves just a little for the task of handling a boat – and surely an element of adventure was to be welcomed in these conforming days? At any rate we warmed all the more to Frank and Kate, who approached adventure with delighted acceptance.

When finally the great day came and we set off from St. Ives for the first short trip round to Newlyn our complement for the holiday consisted of myself and Jess; our younger children Stephen, Demelza, and Genevieve; our 20-year-old son Martin, and 19-year-old daughter Gill, and Gill's boy friend Alan Moss; and Frank and Katie Baker and their daughter – a total of eleven. For the afternoon trip round to Newlyn we also took along two friends, Donald Swan, who had illustrated several of my earlier books, and Dennis Pattison from Pothleven. We knew that Donald had spent several years in the merchant navy and as a result of this experience he had been rather disapproving of our amateur boating exploits. However, we forgave him now as, once on board, he obviously gave way to all his old love of the sea and manifestly enjoyed the short but interesting voyage round by Land's End. For the last couple of hours Donald took over the wheel and regaled us with a stream of advice about sea-going procedures, much of which I was to remember gratefully on the rest of the voyage.

At Newlyn Frank and Josephine were waiting for us; unfortunately Katie's father had been taken ill and she hadn't been able to come down yet, but planned to join us the next day at Salcombe. Later on some friends from Mousehole, Bill and Biddy Pickard, came over bearing a cold chicken and a bottle of wine, so we soon had a very merry gathering down in *Sanu*'s saloon, which for the next fortnight was to be bursting with humanity. Unluckily Jess had begun the trip with a very bad attack of sinus and was confined to her cabin, but apart from this we felt full of gay expectation as at last, after waving goodbye to our visitors, we checked on the ropes and went to bed about midnight, ready for an early morning start.

When we left Newlyn Harbour about eight the next day Mount's Bay was shrouded with mist, and I did not feel altogether easy as I set course for the Lizard, and hoped for the best. However, before we reached the familiar cliffs and lighthouse the mist had risen and brilliant sunshine was pouring down – it had in fact been really a heat haze. From the Lizard I set a new course for Prawle Point, and we were off on a straight line of about sixty miles. This was probably the smoothest and most comfortable part of the whole trip. The water was like glass; occasionally basking sharks popped up and then went away again; now and then we passed some fishing boat or tanker; otherwise we were completely alone with sun and sea. As a present for the boat we had bought one of those battery-operated record players, which had eagerly been taken over by Stephen. Now, across the silence, floated the rather familiar strains of the Beatles lustily singing "Please Please Me", "Love Me Do" and other hits of the moment. Somehow, as so often with the Beatles, it all fitted in, and imparted to us all an extra layer of gaiety. We were off, on our great voyage.

Although the mist had retreated, it hung about not very far away so that it was impossible to see the distant land. I had hoped, as we got into the late afternoon, that I would spy Eddystone lighthouse which would have helped to confirm for me that we were heading approximately in the right direction. Now began the first of several rather amusing spot-the-lighthouse sessions which were to be a feature of the trip. In this Gill's friend Alan usually joined me – both of us developed positive hallucinations that we could see a lighthouse, there on the horizon – there, see? . . . Oh, wait a minute, it seemed to be moving. Oh, dear . . . perhaps it was a ship? . . . Yes, alas, it *was* a ship. It was amazing, that afternoon, how many times Alan and I saw the Eddystone lighthouse, only to be disappointed as it sailed away. Maybe one of our sights had been the real one, but I couldn't be sure, and the mist was beginning to bother me. Supposing my course was out a little, and we missed Prawle Point, and Start Point just beyond it? In that case we might carry on merrily and miss land altogether. Once again, as on a previous occasion, I played safe by bringing *Sanu* several degrees towards the land, and once again this at least had the desired effect. After a while we finally sighted the southern end of Bigbury Bay, and soon found the buoy marking a line to Bolt Head and, just beyond it, Salcombe. Our detour had taken extra time and it was about half past seven when finally we safely crossed the bar into Salcombe estuary. One of the reasons I had picked Salcombe as a stopping place on our way to the Channel Islands was that earlier in the season Geoff Scott had brought us in. Now, with the advantage of remembering that entrance, it wasn't really too difficult to bring *Sanu* down towards the harbour. When we were opposite the Marine Hotel Alan and Stephen let go the anchor (with plenty of chain) and soon we were snug for the night. Not long after two boys in a dinghy brought out the waiting Katie, to complete our crew.

Soon after eight the next morning we were heading out of Salcombe again, this time on a course of about 170° which was calculated to bring us up to Les Hanois Lighthouse, on the west coast of Guernsey, some sixty miles away. It was our first real ocean crossing, and not unnaturally I was beset by worries. In some attempt to offset these I had gone to the trouble of buying a reliable hand-bearing compass, and now as we steamed away from the coastline of Prawle Point and Start Point I got Alan to take periodical bearings. So long as he was able to do this we were able to confirm that we were on the right course, and this was some comfort. But, of course, the farther we travelled, the more we began to get out of sight of land. Fortunately on this particular day visibility was almost startlingly good, and we were able to take bearing on Start Point for nearly twenty miles. As against this advantage, with the bright clear weather came strong blustery winds, estimated on the radio at a probable Force 5, so that almost as soon as we had left the land and until we reached St.

Peter Port we were beset by rough weather. It wasn't overwhelming or frightening, but it was unmistakably rough, and just as certainly increasing in force. The journey was distinctly uncomfortable.

On the other hand we could not help feeling exhilarated at this new experience. We had now lost sight of the mainland and here we were in the middle of the English Channel, bound for "the other side" — alone in a great sea. True the weather was blustery, but otherwise the conditions were stimulating — a warm crisp air, a blue sky and a friendly sun to keep us company. Not that we were ever alone for very long, for we were crossing some of the busy Channel shipping lanes. Almost every time I looked around the horizon I spied a funnel here, a mast there. Most of the ships were going at right angles to us so that there was never much problem of avoidance — usually they were travelling a good deal faster, and I found it quite simple to judge whether to slacken speed or whether I had sufficient clearance. Stephen, of course, had a field day, getting out his binoculars and studying each ship intently. Some of them were quite enormous, especially the new oil tankers with strange structures rising up like huge claws. Such ships left huge white wakes that trailed away for hundreds of feet, making our own seem puny by comparison.

Because of the fairly rough sea I found the job of steering more physically tiring than normal, though over the summer I had mastered the general principle of constantly correcting and allowing for a slight veering one way or another. In fact, steering a boat like *Sanu* can be quite arduous over a lengthy period and no doubt I should have thought about this problem before we set out and given a spot of practice to my crew! Now, while keeping a watchful eye on things, I let various people have a go. It was surprising how difficult each one found it to hold a course of about 170°. In one instance I went for a quick stroll round the deck and came back to find a momentary panic as the wheel had taken charge of the steerer and we were heading back to England! But in fact these are all inevitable teething troubles and all that is required is practice.

Soon after losing sight of the mainland Alan and I began our lighthouse spotting game. Secretly I was afraid I would spot the Casquets lighthouse, which we weren't supposed to see, and the sight of which would mean we were badly off course. More positively Alan looked hopefully for Guernsey. After several occasions of being almost positive we could see Les Hanois, Alan and I lost heart a little, and finally I think it was someone else who actually spotted, on the far horizon, exactly where it should be, the tall shape of the lighthouse, with foam-strewn rocks all around.

Although by now the sea was much rougher I felt peculiarly elated to find that we had actually crossed this no man's land of empty ocean, and come upon our destination exactly. This gave me great new confidence in my compass, for I had never truly before felt able to rely completely on such a minute and simple thing.

But our journey was by no means over, for we had in fact to head out to sea to avoid being carried too near to what it soon became apparent was a peculiarly nasty piece of coastline. A phrase from Adlard Coles, writing about the west coast of Guernsey, stuck in my mind. After describing in some detail numerous "large black rocks" and "low patches" which were strewn about, he commented disarmingly: "Of course, all this interesting part can be avoided by just keeping an offing of 4 miles all the way round." Now, confronted by the awesome looking rock patches themselves, and harried by the regular and increasing rough swell, I followed this good advice, and kept well out of harm's way.

At last we sighted St. Martin's lighthouse marking the southeast corner of Guernsey, and were able to swing round for the last short journey of some two miles up the east coast to St. Peter Port. We were now out of the worst of the rough weather, but it was still quite choppy as, keeping a tense look-out for various beacons, I brought *Sanu* nearer to the now easily recognisable

D*

port, with Castle Cornet towering against the sky line. By now we were all pretty tired and I looked forward to a quick entry and mooring, and a wonderful period of relaxation. It was not to be achieved quite as simply as all that.

Some weeks before setting off I had taken the trouble to write to the harbour master at Guernsey and been assured that by early September the harbour would not be so crowded, and we could rely on having a berth in the inner harbour. I had studied my large-scale map of St. Peter Port diligently and had a rough idea of where the inner harbour would be – but as we came up to the main harbour entrance and I looked into the distance to where the inner harbour should be, all I could see was absolute forest of boats of all shapes and sizes, all anchored in the water off the outer harbour. By now we were level with the first pier-head, and our agitated discussions were broken across by a loud hail on a megaphone, demanding to know who we were and where from and so on. Foolishly I did not immediately mention that we had already written and arranged – after all, gliding into a small harbour in a 61-ft. boat is hardly the time for considered thought! It was only as we were almost past the pier and out of hearing that the man with the megaphone suddenly shouted: "Are you Mr. Baker? Oh, well – there's a berth for you in the inner harbour." By now it was too late for me to ask nervously just which way to the inner harbour. There we were, gliding remorsely towards the packed boats without any clear idea of where we were going.

At this moment, perhaps sensing our predicament, a small motor launch which had come in after us drew level and asked if we wanted help. Somehow our answer must have been misunderstood: the man shouted that if we would follow him he would lead us safely in – and off he set towards a small harbour entrance away on the right, which although it was not where I had expected it to be, I accepted as being the inner harbour. It was no joke steering *Sanu* into such a confined space but I managed it, and we came right up alongside a curiously desolate looking quay.

Frank and Alan jumped ashore and began tying us up, and I was just about to lean over to thank the motor-launch owner, when I became aware of an official in uniform gesticulating angrily.

"You can't stay here. This is a commercial quay. You want the inner harbour." And he pointed over towards the forest of ships.

I looked pathetically across to the man in the motor launch, who fortunately now understood my real destination. Once again, thank goodness, he promised to guide me in. With considerable difficulty we reversed and pulled on ropes and managed to turn *Sanu* round, and I steamed away, forgetting all about Frank and Alan on the quay! I couldn't face trying to reverse back, and they signalled that they would run round to the inner harbour.

At long last I managed to identify the entrance to the inner harbour, which lay beyond the moored boats. Now began the most agonising quarter of an hour of my life as a skipper, for I had to bring *Sanu* down a narrow channel among those moored boats and head for a gap between two stone jetties which hardly seemed much wider than *Sanu* herself. . . . All this somehow I accomplished, just in time to find Alan standing on one of the jetties and shouting that our berth was at the very far corner of the inner harbour, and that to reach it we had to thread our way between a whole new lot of boats already moored inside the harbour. There was just a very narrow channel between the boats anchored in the centre and those lining the quay, and apart from confining my 60 by 18 ft. monster to that channel I also had to make two right-angle turns, one to starboard, the second to port – all in a matter of a minute or so – if presented with the problem on paper or asked in leisurely advance I would have said – "Impossible!" But here and now I had no alterative. *Sanu*'s snub nose was heading straight for some innocent small motor-boat. Swing the wheel hard over, she just comes round . . . now we are aiming straight into the west wall of the quay, but swing her round, and reverse a little, then forward . . . ah, she's creeping round . . . missed it, good, now we are on the home straight, throttle down but not

altogether, better to creep forward and then control by reversing
. . . steadily does it, weave between that mooring rope and the
small yacht, steady, steady – ah, wonder of wonders, there in the
very corner of the harbour is an empty space, obviously meant for
Sanu. But hardly much longer than our own length, and with a
very modern gleaming motor cruiser moored before – mustn't
crush her, whatever I do, that would not be a good arrival. . . .
Fortunately Alan and Frank were standing there on the quay, so
we threw them ropes, and got the bow of the boat tied up, and then
threw the ropes back to where we found one of the friendly
fellows on the motor-boat had come ashore to give a hand. By
now quite a crowd had gathered to watch our arrival: well at
least we had come to a full stop, and in our berth! Now, gradually
we pulled on the ropes, and slowly, awkwardly, *Sanu* was pulled
in – until at long, long last we were in our berth and I could go
down and shut off the engine.

Somehow, once we were safely tied up and secure also in the
knowledge that we needn't move for several days, all my weari-
ness and worry seemed to vanish. Indeed, all of us suddenly
plucked up new spirits, and began smiling and talking away. And
small wonder, for here we were on a lovely September evening,
moored in the centre of what appeared a beautiful little harbour.
Our berth left us with our bow actually facing the pavement of the
main street of St. Peter Port, with the curiously continental-
looking houses and shops rising up steeply away from us. The first
lights were beginning to twinkle, and all around us rose the steep
masts of yachts and other boats, and over on the other quays one
could see the large shapes of steamers. It was all strange and new
and very stimulating. Even as we sat around recovering our composure we saw two very high masts looming on the skyline and a
few moments later watched a lovely old-time ketch, with full-rig,
edging into the harbour, performing in fact the same feat that we
had just accomplished, only by the look of it in the hands of someone more familiar with the harbour layout. She came nearly as far

as us, and then tied up next to a moored boat – not long after her skipper came over and had a chat. He was a local man who had bought the boat almost as scrap and spent a year working to bring her back to her original condition. Some day he planned to take her on a world cruise.

St. Peter Port, we found, was full of characters like that. Many of the local boat owners chartered their boats in the summer, and went off on their own down south in the winter months. It was a busy bustling place; and the town likewise. We liked particularly the continental atmosphere, noticeable in the winding alleyways, and in such impressive institutions as the spotlessly clean market place where the next morning we indulged ourselves in buying large quantities of fresh fruit and vegetables – especially of course, tomatoes!

On returning from this shopping expedition we were confronted on the quayside by two men, one carrying an expensive looking camera, who turned out to be reporter and photographer from the local newspaper, the *Guernsey Star*. By a coincidence, an article of mine about our experiences of buying *Sanu* had recently appeared in *Motor Boat and Yachting*, and in fact someone had just been reading it when they had seen the very same boat sail into harbour! Now they wanted a story for the next day's paper.

We were rather amused at this unforeseen limelight, especially when the next day the story appeared on the front page of the newspaper with a large photograph of the whole crew of *Sanu* and the headline: BOATLOAD OF ARTISTS. This was not the end of the matter, either, for a similar story and yet another photograph appeared that day in the evening newspaper – while that same afternoon a smart young man from Channel Television arrived, complete with television camera. This, of course, thrilled the children who proceeded to drape themselves about in fetching attitudes looking more like child models than sailors. There was even, we were told later, an item broadcast in the B.B.C. West Region

News, that the Val Bakers had arrived safely at St. Peter Port, Guernsey, in their M.F.V. *Sanu*. This quite cheered us, showing that our fate would not have gone unnoticed if anything untoward had happened.

Unfortunately for the children we were unable to watch our début on Channel Television as when the programme was shown we had gone to the island of Herm, about two miles across from St. Peter Port. Jess had been indignantly insistent that we should go across in our two small dinghies, as befitting people with boats of their own, but I knew from my study of the charts that even that short stretch of sea – it was after all the notorious Little Russell Channel – could be quite dangerous, and I didn't fancy being caught in it in such small craft. Consequently we went across in one of the powerful motor-launches that run regularly backwards and forwards. During the journey, as the waves rose high and the spray flew all over us, I was thankful I had been so insistent.

Herm lived up to all the pleasant tales we had heard about it – quite literally a dream island, and very reminiscent to us of some of the Scilly islands. About one-and-a-half miles long it is lined with lovely sandy beaches, the best known of these being the famous shell beach whose "sand" is composed of billions of tiny fragments of shells mixed with whole shells. Like the Scilly island, Tresco, we discovered, Herm is in the tenancy of one man, Major Peter Wood, who has organised it deliberately to cater for the holiday visitors and, it seemed to us, with good taste and great practicality. Apart from the natural beauties of the beaches and inland walks such as the one through a grove of rhododendron bushes and gum trees to the medieval farm building, there are useful amenities – a pub, hotel and restaurant, and several very handy beach cafés. The island runs its own farm herd and market gardens, and operates a commercial bulb growing business, as well as several crafts, such as pottery, knitted wear and shell jewellery. Along with Lundy Island, off the Devon coast, Herm also has its own stamp printings, which have a big souvenir sale.

We all enjoyed our few hours on Herm, beginning with drinks in the gardens of the "Mermaid", and ending with sunbathing on the shell beach and our first bathe of the trip, duly recorded on the ciné camera, and ending with a cliff-top walk round to catch the boat back from Rosiere Steps. We felt truly away from it all, and were half sorry when the powerful motor-launch chugged its way back into St. Peter Port, not long before dusk.

Back on *Sanu* we found a surprise waiting for us in the form of a scribbled note pinned to the door of the wheelhouse. This turned out to be a message from some friends, Jack and Pepe Gillies, who when last heard of were living in Malaga, Spain. They had read about our arrival in the *Guernsey Star* and now gave us their telephone number and asked us round for a drink. This was one of those unexpected touches that make boat trips even more delightful. The previous evening Jess and I had tried the experiment of taking the entire crew out for a meal at a local hotel, and apart from the alarming cost it had demonstrated that there are times when it is better to separate the children from the adults. Here was our opportunity. That evening Jess and I and Frank and Katie slipped away to call on the Gillies, who had left Malaga and come almost by chance to live at Guernsey, which they found cheap and pleasant in many ways, but ultimately rather boring. Whereas we were full of the island's first impact, always a pleasing one as they admitted, they were thinking nostalgically of their earlier life in Cornwall and plying us with questions about cottages for sale. We had a very convivial evening drinking and chatting until the small hours, when Jack, who had just returned from scripting several television plays in America, ran us back to *Sanu* by moonlight.

"Well," he said thoughtfully, after being shown round the boat, "you've really disturbed me. We've been thinking of moving again, either back to Cornwall or maybe somewhere like Portugal. But now I'm beginning to wonder – perhaps we might do better to buy a boat like this!"

8

A Night to Remember

AFTER four days at St. Peter Port we were all set for a morning departure when suddenly the whole of Guernsey and the surrounding waters was enveloped by mist; all aircraft were grounded and the Channel packet steamer from Weymouth was hours late. I had read about this tendency affecting the Channel Islands but was unprepared for the speed of change. We waited for that day in harbour, and then when the next morning dawned bright and clear we busied ourselves turning *Sanu* round by ropes in the confined space so that the bow was headed towards the harbour exit. Just as we had started our engine and were moving off – down came the beginnings of another mist. However, it didn't as yet seem as bad as the previous day, and as our journey was a fairly short one of about eight miles across to Sark, and we could as yet still see the island over on our port, I decided to carry on.

In my armchair studies of charts and maps I had assessed every little detail about Sark and decided the best anchorage would be a sheltered spot on the west coast called Havre Gosselin. After all wasn't it the great Adlard Coles's own favourite spot? "A deep and good anchorage in fine weather with clean bottom. . . ." Unfortunately, as it happened, I had mentioned my intention to one of the friendly local boat owners at St. Peter Port, a man I knew to have taken his boat in and out of every cove in the district. His reaction was a dubious shake of the head.

"Havre Gosselin's exposed to the west – and the prevailing wind is west. Take my tip, you head for Bec du Nez and once you're round there take a bearing on Pointe Robert lighthouse — just before that you'll find a lovely anchorage at La Greve de la Ville. It's completely sheltered from any westerlies."

So it was, indeed. We came round the headland and at once recognised the white tip of Pointe Robert. There was a yacht already anchored close to the shore so we edged in quietly and dropped our anchor about a hundred yards farther out. The mist had risen, the sun shone brilliantly, all around us tall cliffs formed a comforting shelter from any wanton winds of the west. . . . Oh, yes it was a lovely spot. In the afternoon we lowered our two dinghies and ran ashore and then climbed up steep cliff pathways alive with colour and fragrance, primroses and heather and golden gorse . . . when we looked back from the top there was *Sanu* lying peacefully at anchor in the centre of the small bay, just like some idyllic scene one imagined on a tropical island. We took photographs and walked on to explore the tiny lanes and byways of Sark, ending up in the quaint narrow main street which is possibly crowded with visitors at the height of the season but now was mercifully peaceful. We were intrigued to learn from the jovial lady in the grocery stores that her name was the good old Cornish one of Lanyon, and that she came in fact from Redruth, and that quite a few Cornish families had settled in Sark at the time when there was a silver mine in operation.

We were even more intrigued to follow the winding lane down to the twin harbours of La Maseline and Le Creux, each approached by a tunnel in the cliffs and opening out rather like some incredible film set. There are no cars at all on Sark, but on the way down to the harbour we passed several examples of the main form of alternative transport — horse-drawn hansom cabs with their bowler hatted cabbies sitting upright holding the reins.

"Tomorrow," said Jess firmly, "we must all have a ride on one of those."

But tomorrow was to be a different sort of day. It began marvellously enough, a blazing sun beating down on the picturesque bay so that the water, cool and greeny-blue and so clear you could see the bottom, proved an irresistible attraction. Before breakfast Frank was having a dip, soon to be joined by most of the others. Ah, this was the life — this was cruising as it should be! I had the ciné camera out and one by one took the children diving in, and having a race over to the nearby yacht and back. Just after they had finished I noticed the crew of the other boat making preparations to depart, but thought nothing more of it at the time. Too late, I was to learn respect for their acumen.

It was such a lovely day that we decided to spend it exploring parts of Sark we had not yet seen. In particular, both Frank and I were intrigued to see that there was a Baker's Valley, and planned to include this in our route. Once again we rowed ashore in the two dinghies and left them high up on the beach, safe until the next high tide, which was due about the time we expected to come back.

Once ashore it was rather similar to the previous day. We wandered through pretty lanes, and, after having a drink sitting comfortably in deck chairs outside the main island pub, we picked up some food and set off down through Baker's Valley, which provided a beautiful walk leading down to a smooth sandy beach curling round what was known as Dixcart Bay. Here we lazed away the early part of the afternoon, explored the caves, and had another swim . . . it was all quite heavenly and away from it all.

Next we followed the winding cliff path until we reached one of the island's showpieces, La Coupée, which joins Sark to Little Sark. This is a natural causeway of rock nearly 300 feet high and 415 feet long, across which runs a road just wide enough for a horse and cart to cross (about nine feet). Like the other Channel Islands, Sark was occupied by the Germans during the war and afterwards they in turn became prisoners, and it was these men who helped to erect the road, directed by our own Royal Engineers. It is certainly a strange and rather awe-inspiring spot, from which you can see clearly along both coastlines. It would only have required a sight of the reigning La Dame, "often to be seen riding her bicycle along the dusty roads" according to the local guide-books, to complete a bizarre experience.

We did not see La Dame—but we did notice for the first time, as we turned to begin the long walk back to La Greve de la Ville, a subtle change in the atmosphere. From somewhere a wind had sprung up, ruffling the hedge tops and bending the trees—nothing startling at first, but unmistakably increasing in strength. The sun still shone, but there was a slightly less friendly feeling about things, somehow. And worst of all, I frowned to myself and held up a wet finger. There could be no denying it—the wind was blowing not from the west, but from the very opposite, the east. And that was the one direction to which our snug little anchorage was exposed.

It was a long walk back to the cliffs above La Greve and nearly seven o'clock in the evening by the time we reached there, by now rather tired. The moment I came on top of the steep cliff path all my worst fears were realised. What had begun as a slight breeze was now a blustery wind, blowing in directly on to the shore. The sea in which we had bathed this morning so peacefully was suddenly turned into what with very little exaggeration might be called a seething cauldron.

As we descended the steep cliff path in glum silence I took stock of our rather alarming position. Some way out in the middle of the bay our beloved travelling home, *Sanu*, was at anchor, though she would hardly be said to be resting: big as she was, she was tossing up and down like a helpless toy. Even being aboard *Sanu* it was going to be quite uncomfortable—and we were by no means aboard. We still had to make a trip of a couple of hundred yards in two tiny dinghies, in the face of large waves and a huge swell.

It was, to date, undoubtedly the worst moment of the whole trip. We began to gather on the beach where I was further dismayed to find waves breaking on the stony shore rather as they did at Porthmeor at home, with full surfing force. Still, there was

nothing for it but to have a go. First Martin and Gill and I got the smaller dinghy ready, with Demelza and Josephine already aboard. Heading the bow to the oncoming waves, we pushed it out, and Martin and Gill jumped aboard. On this occasion they managed to clear the shore reasonably, and we then watched in an agony of apprehension as they rowed out — each wave, it seemed, threatening to over-turn the tiny boat. Somehow, though, they managed to reach *Sanu* — there to face the considerable problem of how to get aboard, since one moment the little dinghy was almost above *Sanu*, the next the bigger ship was looming menacingly high above the dinghy. Fortunately we had several old motor car tyres hanging over the side as fenders, and Martin and Gill found that by holding on to these they were able to make it possible for the other two girls to get aboard. Then, knowing that in such a rough sea one person might not be able to manage, they both stayed in the boat and rowed ashore again.

Now we decided that Martin and Gill and Genevieve and I should make the next trip in the dinghy, leaving the others to come over in the large fibre-glass dinghy. This time we were not so lucky in our get-away. Before we could even get Genny aboard, with Martin and I trying to hold the dinghy bow fast, a great wave appeared and half submerged the boat so that we had to hastily drag it ashore again. The only way now was to put Genny and Gill aboard and for Martin and I to wade out holding the boat steady, and then, immediately we had survived one wave, to give a shove and jump aboard. Somehow we managed it in the end . . . and then ensued one of the most terrifying journeys of my life, ending with the equally alarming experience of trying to hold on to a pulsating, almost bestial *Sanu*, leaping and plunging about.

At last, miraculously, we were aboard, and for the time being tied the dinghy on a long line at the back. Now there remained the formidable journey of the larger dinghy, containing Frank and Kate, Jess and Stephen, and Alan. We watched their several attempts to launch the boat into the beating waves. At last they managed to scramble aboard and get away — only, so we later realised, to find that in the general mix-up the two people in charge of the oars, Frank and Kate, had probably the least rowing experience. It was too late in such turbulent conditions, and in a rather overcrowded boat, to make any changes. There then ensued ten minutes or more of apprehensive waiting as we watched the tossing dinghy slowly and rather haphazardly being brought across the bay. Sometimes it seemed to go off course altogether; at other times it almost headed back: while aboard *Sanu*, I was shouting futilely into the wind, and those on the dinghy were shouting back with equal futility, neither of us hearing a word. Every now and then an extra large wave would come along that would, to us watching from *Sanu*, seem to pick up the dinghy and threaten to hurtle it and its occupants back on to the beach.

But by a miracle and the fairly reliable law of buoyancy as applied to the construction of a good dinghy, disaster was survived.

At long last the bigger dinghy reached the side of *Sanu* — there to be poised for a few more moments in horrifying up-and-down motion, until at last those aboard were able to pull themselves aboard, and we tied that dinghy up at the back as well.

We were a very chastened crew that gathered on the rolling deck. For of course, far from being over, our troubles were now in full spate. The wind was blowing up more strongly than ever, and our first job must be to haul in the dinghies — an operation which at the best of times involves several people, one of whom was to be down in the dinghy attaching ropes. The hero of this hazardous occasion was Alan, and he must have spent nearly an hour being tossed about in one dinghy after another before finally the job was accomplished.

Now began what was truly to prove a long day's journey into the night. In conditions of familiarity I might have been tempted to sail away from such an unhealthy situation, but by now darkness had fallen and we were surrounded by a motley collection of evil looking rocks with names such as La Petite Moie, Moire Pierre and Pavlaison (the latter, ominously, only awash at low water). I felt we had better stay where we were until daylight, so there was nothing left really but to settle down to an uncomfortable night.

Uncomfortable, I should say, for the crew. For the skipper I can honestly say it was the most alarming and apprehensive night of my short life at sea — worse even than the one at St. Ives. Our anchorage was surrounded on three sides by tall cliffs at whose edge the presence of fierce rock fangs were evidenced by the white foam breaking . . . only a matter of 200 yards or so separated us from the shore in three directions — and, from the fourth, the waves were bearing down on us directly.

It was impossible for me to think of sleep. For hour after hour during the night I followed a pattern of behaviour. First every few minutes I stared out fixedly at the one useful point of reference, the nearby light of Pointe Robert lighthouse: as long as I could see this, I felt we were reasonably safe, even though of course with changes of the tide we sometimes moved around. Next I would take a walk round the boat trying to check on our distance to various points on the shore, which loomed up with strange menace. Finally I went to the bow and leaned over staring in an agony of apprehension at the taut chain. Would it hold? My hypnotic contemplation of that slender thread that alone held *Sanu* and her eleven passengers safe from the waiting cliffs was not helped by the occasional movement of horror when an extra large wave hit the boat and she positively leaped into the air, so it seemed, pulling the chain with her, giving it a sudden vicious extra strain.

So it went on, that nightmare night. Every few minutes I would go into our deck cabin and sit uneasily, watching the lighthouse through a porthole, addressing all my fears and neuroses to poor Jess . . . then deciding suddenly that the anchor must be dragging and rushing out. At various intervals during the night I would encounter another shadowy figure that was Frank, unable to sleep like myself, and we would exchange commiserations.

"And to think what a beautiful day it was," commented Frank sadly.

Beautiful day it had been, and hideous night it now was—but day and night have their end, and at long last the first wispy light of dawn began to colour the horizon. By this fragile light I took a good look and found that though we had indeed survived the night, we must have dragged a very small amount, for we were undoubtedly nearer the cliffs than before. However, enough was enough.

"Wake up. We're moving—NOW!"

Miraculously the engine started without hesitation, and I ran to take the wheel, shouting out:

"Raise the anchor, then."

From my point of view it was quite a tricky operation to get the boat away from her present position. I had to be ready to open the throttle slowly as soon as the anchor showed signs of breaking.

Consequently I paid scant attention to what was going on around the winch, where Alan, Martin and Frank were turning handles and hauling up. Suddenly there was a bit of commotion and a cry and to my astonishment I saw Frank stagger back, with blood pouring from a cut in the head. At that precise moment there was nothing to be done but make sure we got the boat safely away, and this we managed in the next few minutes. The anchor finally came up, and I headed between those two ominous rocks, and at long happy last, set a course that took us safely away from Sark and its now nightmare memories, and bound for Jersey.

Only then did I dare relax to attend to Frank, and we found to our concern that he was quite badly shaken. Apparently the handle of the winch had jumped off and hit him on the head, or rather would have done if he had not raised a hand to take the full force. Unfortunately, it was to transpire that he had in fact broken a finger; but for the moment it seemed mostly a general shaking, and Kate took him down to bed and got him to rest.

So we headed for Jersey, the largest and best known of the Channel Islands. Originally I had assumed we would make for St. Helier, the main port, but since then I had been studying with some alarm the large-scale Admiralty Chart, from which the approach to St. Helier appeared to be through a labyrinth of evil-looking rocks. Closer reading of Adlard Coles produced one or two straws in the wind: "Navigation in the coast of South East Jersey calls for greater experience and caution than elsewhere. . . ." On the other hand: "Gorey is a charming little town nestling under Mont Orgueil . . . the only port other than St. Helier where customs can be cleared . . . many yachtsmen prefer it to the larger port." Conversation with friends on Guernsey who knew the Jersey coast well confirmed a sneaking suspicion that perhaps we might be happier in a pretty, small harbour. So I decided Gorey should be our destination.

This meant now that instead of keeping west and heading for La Corbière lighthouse, our course took us down between the

Paternosters and the Dirouilles, two straggling reefs of large rocks which were pretty easy to identify and avoid. . . . Almost from the time we left Sark it was possible to see the humped coastline of Jersey, about twenty miles away. It was a sunny morning, and now that we were out at sea we didn't seem so badly affected by the rough weather, which in any case began to abate. Soon it was possible to see the white-washed rock known as Tour de Rozel, and we altered course to follow the north coast of Jersey round to Gorey, on the north-east. We had made good time and I confidently expected we would soon be safe in Gorey Harbour, but I had reckoned without the extremely strong tidal streams. For a while, with *Sanu*'s 88 horse-power engines flat out, we barely seemed to move against the coastline. It took us about three-quarters of an hour to travel from Rozel round St. Catherine breakwater, a distance of less than three miles! Just on this point, too, we had the added discomfort of a swell coming across our bows, but we were cheered now by seeing the dramatic silhouette of Mont Orgueil, and knew that journey's end was not far. The approach to Gorey appeared a little tricky, with beacons popping out of the water all over the place. I knew I had to avoid the buoy marking Les Arch Rocks, and giving it a good wide berth brought *Sanu* round until the quay of Gorey lay directly ahead, and we edged in quietly to find calm waters, and several interested spectators, and a most friendly harbour master who on hearing of Frank's accident immediately rang up a doctor to come and check up.

Gorey was everything one could wish for: a picturesque pleasant harbour, friendly people, and complete shelter from the outside weather. As it was also only a twenty-minute bus journey from St. Helier we were not really cut off — and it only required one journey in that bus, which followed the coastline, for me to feel like offering up fervent prayers of deliverance. True it was low tide when we made the journey, but the fact remained that the low level of water revealed an absolute forest of hideous looking rocks with jagged tips rising high, many of them lying just below the surface at high tide. The prospect of bringing *Sanu* anywhere near this St. Helier jungle would have been absolutely horrifying.

During our stay on Guernsey we had managed, by hiring a mini-bus for the day, to cram in quite an illuminating tour of the island. Not, as it happened, a very encouraging one. Although we liked St. Peter Port, and found one or two pretty bays on the south coast, it seemed to us that most of Guernsey was over-built, indeed it seemed in danger of becoming one enormous suburb. Now, when we decided to repeat the experiment and hired another mini-bus on Jersey, we were apprehensive of finding the same sort of conditions. Our pessimism was unfounded: from the moment we left St. Helier and reached the pretty resort of St. Aubin we were all very impressed with the beauty of the Jersey coast and country. We had lunch at St. Brelade Bay, whose broad sweep and surfing sands reminded us very much of Cornwall — then on to something even more nostalgic, the wonderful wild and rugged peninsula of La Corbière, with its famous lighthouse and causeway. Surely we were back in Cornwall? So it went on. All along the west and north coast of Jersey we kept discovering lovely little coves like Plemont, Greve de Lecq, Bonne Nuit Bay, Bouley Bay and Rozel — every one of them surprisingly unspoiled. And as a contrast to them there was St. Ouen's, the largest beach in the Channel Islands, extending along the whole of the west coast.

Like Frank and Kate, Jess and I were fascinated by all this varied scenery, but it has to be admitted the children found a more overriding interest. While on Guernsey we accidentally discovered a thriving Go Kart track, and the children became wildly bitten by the craze. Now, near St. Brelade, we found an even bigger and more exciting track where (at 1s. a minute!) they proceeded to indulge in their motor-racing fantasies. The experience was so amusing, and the profitability obviously so enormous, that ever since we have carried in the back of our minds the notion that surely if somewhere in West Cornwall a track could be started. . . .?

Back at Gorey we also paid our dutiful cultural visit to the imposing remains of Mont Orgueil Castle, which was actually begun by the Normans in the tenth century on the site of Caesar's Camp. At one time Sir Walter Raleigh was the Governor, and during its long history the castle has been the centre of many fierce battles, notably during the Civil War when it was captured by the Parliamentarians after a long siege. A tableaux complete with poetic recitation and weird luminating effects, taught us something we did not know—that here in 1781 was fought the last battle on British soil, against the French. The castle had also in its time harboured many famous prisoners, among them William Prynne, imprisoned there for his opposition to King Charles. We were intrigued to learn that he arrived by boat from Caernarvon in North Wales after "an adventurous voyage of 14 weeks"—compared to our own voyage of more than half that distance in under a week.

In fact, of course, the distance direct from Jersey to Cornwall is about 150 miles and now, through circumstances beyond our control we were going to achieve a considerable reduction in the time of such a journey. Originally I had planned that we would make our return journey via Alderney, with a stay of a day or two on this most northerly of the Islands. I had heard a lot about the dreaded Alderney Race, where currents of six or seven knots might have to be faced, and frankly was not looking forward to the encounter. Still, I was manfully preparing—and then the weather reports began to speak of Forces 7 and 8 and "gales imminent". Faced with the choice of risking such conditions *and* the Alderney Race, or staying snug in Gorey Harbour, we chose the latter!

By the time the gales abated, and we had a chance to move, our holiday period was reduced to two days, and after some hesitation I made the obvious remaining choice. We would sail *Sanu* direct from Gorey to Newlyn in Cornwall, a distance of about 150 miles — at least twice as far as any previous journey we had made. With a cruising speed of about seven knots, it was a simple matter of calculation to work out that, no matter how early we started, the latter part of our journey would have to be carried out under the unwelcome cloak of darkness.

It would be our first taste of night navigation. Looking back, it is difficult now to understand why one of us didn't have the bright and simple idea of planning the time-table so that the night-time was spent in the comparative safety of open sea, and departure and arrival would thus occur in the comforting daylight. However, these are things one usually only learns by bitter experience. Added to this major worry we also had a niggling doubt — how about the Kelvin engine? It had carried us valiantly on a number of trips to Plymouth, Fowey, the Isles of Scilly and now the Channel Islands without faltering; but none of these trips had taken more than about ten hours. How would the old war-horse respond to a period of more than double its previous record? Again, being comparative novices, we didn't appreciate that a good diesel will go on for ever, provided it is properly maintained. And I'm glad to say that the faithful Kelvin pounded away relentlessly without a moment's hesitation for some twenty-three hours.

I had worked out a simple enough passage — to follow the Jersey coast from Gorey round to the west side and then set a course of 301° for the Lizard. We set our alarm for an hour before dawn so that by the time the first light was illuminating our passage out of Gorey we had the boat all ship-shape and the engine running; then it was a comparatively easy matter to reverse out and follow the marks to clear us of a number of rather nasty rocks, a task I should not have fancied in the dark.

From about six in the morning until dusk, around eight at night, we were in the open sea, in conditions uncomfortable enough to justify the midnight forecast of Force 5. From time to time a brave spirit ventured below to make a cup of tea or some soup, but in general we did not feel very hungry! And as the long day began to darken, we tended to huddle together in the wheel-house, contemplating a little dubiously the orange-gold sky ahead of us.

This was perhaps my first surprise as, holding the wheel firmly so that the compass registered as steady a 301° as was possible in a rolling sea, I prepared to steer *Sanu* through our first night-passage: the weird and rather disturbing effects of sunset in the western sky. For our course was heading for the sun – or what was left of it. Now, as I stared ahead anxious to make the most of the remaining light, I became confused by the extraordinary sequence of colour patterns – first a deep orange, then (as small clouds moved over the dying rays) a mirage of dozens of small islands. Not long after, the illuminated clouds amalgamated to form an outline of cliffs so realistic that I kept saying hopefully: "Perhaps we've come faster than we realised and we can actually see the Lizard?" Alas, a quick look at the Walker log unfolding at the stern proved this to be an impossibility.

In fact it was another three or four hours before the now pitch-black sky ahead of us was broken for the first time by the three quick flashes of the Lizard lighthouse. I think we all gave a small cheer then, for this meant we had hit our objective in a pretty straight line. Here came my second lesson in night-travel at sea – it's likely to be a long, long way between seeing and finding. I don't mean that we were ever in any doubt about the general whereabouts of the Lizard. What bothered me (and more so, of course, as I was by now very tired, having been at the wheel almost without a break for some fifteen hours) was the difficulty I had in estimating just how near we were to the lighthouse itself. Remem-ber, this was my very first experience of navigation by night. Some-times as I stared ahead desperately trying to pierce the darkness it seemed as if we were almost upon the Lizard. Once indeed, through some kind of momentary hallucination, I even became convinced I could see the cliff-top around the lighthouse and the shape of dark houses — whereas in truth, as Jess firmly pointed out after a lengthy check on the Walker log and the time, we were still perhaps twenty miles away! Intellectually I agreed, but emotionally I remained disturbed, being haunted by a daytime memory of passing the Lizard and seeing those angry rocks: supposing we came upon them before I could steer clear? Haunted by this horrifying vision, I finally gave in to my fears and, probably about ten miles before we really reached the Lizard, played safe by steering a more westerly course so as, in my own mind, to make quite sure that we missed the rocks.

Of course, the result was a minor disaster: we quickly became really off-course; the Lizard kept appearing in different positions, so that it became difficult to estimate which way we should be going. In the end we wasted a whole hour in trying to rectify matters. At last we managed to get on a reasonable course again, and after what seemed an eternity that cursed flashing light began to fall behind us as we headed into Mount's Bay. But even now our troubles were not over, for it was still very, very dark; the time was about 3 o'clock in the morning, and there would be no more lighthouses to aim at, only the lights of Penzance and Newlyn harbours.

And where were they? I peered with sore eyes to right and left, matters not being helped by the arrival of a faint drizzle. By now not merely I, but the other members of our party, were understandably edgy; we differed volubly about what course to follow or what the various distant lights portended. In the end reason prevailed. From that blessed nautical bible, *Reeds*, we had verified that Newlyn Pier light flashed every five seconds, and there it was flashing away. I steered grimly for that last objective, but by now tiredness was sweeping over me in great waves; I found that I was seeing lights and shapes that weren't there, and I had grave doubts whether I should ever manage to bring the boat safely to harbour. Thank goodness I had companions to sustain my spirits; and, thanks to them, at long weary last, just as a cold grey light of another dawn was falling on the sea behind us, I steered *Sanu* through the narrow neck of Newlyn Harbour and up to the nearest vacant patch of quayside. Five minutes later and we could have made a more comfortable entry by daylight – a lesson I intend never to forget!

9

The Winter's Tale

THE awful responsibility of owning a boat of your own is certainly emphasised when you appear to be heading direct for a harbour wall or, with dragging anchor, to be drifting on to some particularly wicked-looking rocks . . . on the other hand we were to find this same awareness even more devastatingly brought home at what might hopefully be regarded as a time of peace: namely, the winter lay-up.

After returning in comparative triumph from our 500-mile trip to the Channel Islands it would have been an obvious anticlimax to have attempted any further short trips – and anyway it would soon be October and the weather was becoming more blustery. Indeed, immediately after our departure from the Channel Islands the equinox storms arrived, resulting in the loss of a 50-ft. motor cruiser and four of her crew, the fifth being miraculously saved after clinging to a piece of wreckage for twenty-four hours. We knew the area where the boat had been in trouble, and the shore where the girl was washed up, and shuddered at our memories of those cruel rocks.

Ah, well, perhaps it was time to bed *Sanu* for the winter! But exactly where? We had a hundred and one things we wanted to do to the boat, from painting to rearranging the interior layout, and it was ridiculous to contemplate a fifty-mile drive to Falmouth and back every time we felt like putting in a couple of hours. At the moment she was tied up at St. Ives quay, but one bad ground swell might do untold damage.

E

Obviously there was only one possible place, and that was Hayle
Estuary across St. Ives bay, where most of the St. Ives fishing
boats put in, even during the summer. Once, Hayle had been a
very busy port, but the existence of a sand bar across its entrance
had been partly responsible for a decline in trade. There was still
a regular traffic of coal and scrap boats which came in on one tide
and usually left on the next after unloading. Most of these large
boats followed the narrow channel that wound up past the big
electricity works and into the town of Hayle itself, where there
were commercial wharves. However, about a couple of hundred
yards inside the sand bar there was a fork in the river, and the
narrow right-hand channel led up to an old disused quay known as
Lelant Quay. Like St. Ives harbour, this quay dried out at low
tide, but the bottom was reasonably flat, with a mixture of shingle
and sand, and there was room alongside for several large boats.
Unlike Hayle it was not on the farther side of the river, but on the
St. Ives side, and no more than ten minutes by car from our house.

Here, then, we decided to make *Sanu's* winter home. We had
moored sometimes at the quay during the summer and knew that
it was seldom used because the fishing boats preferred to go into
Hayle where they could unload their catch direct to waiting lorries.
When we brought *Sanu* over from St. Ives we assumed that we
would have the quay to ourselves, and it was momentarily dis-
quieting, as we crept slowly between marking posts, up the very
narrow channel, to spy the masts of two other ships already moored
there. Naturally they had chosen the best positions, and there was
nothing for us to do but cautiously edge our way rather farther up
than we had been before. We tied up above the second of the
boats, a M.F.V. like ours belonging to a Lamorna man who, we
later learned, had been half way round the world in her. This was
Flowing Tide — the other boat was one of the best-known St. Ives
fishing boats, the *Sweet Promise* which was having a refit.

Once tied up at the quay we put down our outside leg, made
sure that we had plenty of old motor car tyres lining the side

against the quay, and went off home. The next day I came back at the time of low tide just to check up that *Sanu* was settling down reasonably well. It was just as well I did – for I found our beloved boat tilting away from the quay at an alarming angle, only saved from toppling over by the one sturdy leg! What had happened was that, while the bottom around the quay was flat at the seaward end, farther up it shelved away so that in fact there was no flat surface for the leg to rest on, and it only touched ground after tilting down some distance. If we had not put out a leg, the boat would have gone over on its side.

Nothing could be done until the tide came in again. I went home and collected Gill and Jess – unfortunately Stephen was away – and we drove back around high tide. My idea was that we would simply pull the boat back nearer to the other boats, as I had worked out that by so doing we would be back on the flat part. But I had underestimated the strength needed; we pulled and pushed and shoved, but the only result was the rather alarming one that having loosened the rear rope, *Sanu*'s flat bottom was swinging perilously out into mid-stream. There was nothing for it but to start up the engine, with all those laborious procedures; and at last, with the aid of the engine, and Jess and Gill manoeuvring the ropes on the quayside, we managed to move *Sanu* back those vital few feet. We were rather near to the stern of *Flowing Tide*, but then, we noticed, she in turn was close on to the *Sweet Promise*: and in fact the three of us spent several quiet and trouble-free months moored in this positions.

Our first job, self-evidently, would be to clean and paint *Sanu*'s hull. When we had acquired her the Falmouth boatyard manager had congratulated us on our "good bottom", but since then we had accumulated a formidable amount of weed and barnacles. I had never been quite able to comprehend that it is possible, but I am assured that the presence of these flimsy substances on the hull can knock a knot off the boat's speed. Well now, when the tide was out, it was easy to walk under the huge fat hull and the barnacles alone ran into hundreds. There was nothing for it but to drive across to the Fisherman's Co-operative at Newlyn and purchase several large cans of red anti-fouling paint and half a dozen scrapers.

Thus armed, one Sunday, we descended on the quay, along with several of Stephen's friends – the latter a great help, for we found that the children could get underneath *Sanu*'s hull without much trouble, whereas Jess and I could only reach it lying on our backs. The whole job was a painfully drawn-out one, for we were dealing with a hull 60 ft. long and 18 ft. wide. First we had to pass down the hull with the scrapers, wearily hacking off the weed and barnacles. Then we had to go round with putty, looking for any possible cracks or crevices, though I was relieved to find the hull seemed in excellent condition. Finally there came the onslaught with paint brushes and the red anti-fouling – a tedious, seemingly never-ending task at the end of which, inevitably, we were almost as covered in paint as the boat. Still, miraculously, after two or three such visits, *Sanu*'s hull was finished, a gleaming rusty red – and free of weed and barnacles for some time to come.

Once the hull had been tackled, we did not feel so bad, as the remaining work would at least be on board, and even if the weather stopped us painting there was plenty to do below deck. In fact, as it was autumn – a *Cornish* autumn, which can be quite heavenly – we were able to tackle painting the whole of the sides of the deck, and finally the deck itself. Previously it had been painted a light green colour, and since this would not really go with our planned blue and white exterior, we decided to paint the deck a rusty-red. Our original intention was to use a material called Dekaplex, which is waterproof and gives weather protection to the cabins below. When we went to buy some they were out of stock, but they did have in some red lead paint of the same colour which they recommended. Much to our subsequent regret, to save wasting time Jess and I brought back two gallons of the stuff. It did not take us long to paint it on, and the resulting effect was most pleasing. Off we went, feeling very satisfied with ourselves . . . only to return after three days to find, to our dismay, that the paint was still tacky and soft. We felt instinctively things were not as they should be, but went away and gave it another three days. When we came back, there was hardly any change.

Jess and I looked at each other in dismay.

"Supposing it *never* dries?" I said.

When we asked one or two supposedly knowledgeable friends they were even inclined to agree that this was a possibility, and our spirits sank to zero. We decided to make a great effort and leave the boat alone for two whole weeks. Meantime, I wrote off to the Dekaplex Company—and of course we soon realised what had happened. The previous Dekaplex surface was a plastic one, which admitted nothing, whereas paint usually soaks into the substance it is put on—the red copper was unable to do this!

Fortunately our worst fears were not realised. After two more weeks there was a slight but unmistakable improvement, and after that, resigning ourselves to the very slowest progress, we found that very gradually the paint did dry—so that after two months it could be said to have dried off. Finally we were able to apply the new coat of Dekaplex.

After that we turned our attention to the interior of *Sanu*. Ever since we had first acquired her we had felt very strongly that for a boat of her size the saloon was a little on the small side. We had enlarged it slightly by knocking down a partition to the galley, but we had found during the Channel Isles trip that the confinement could be irritating with a large party.

Adjoining the saloon was quite a large bathroom, an unexpected luxury on such a boat—and the fact was that no one had ever used the bath, for of course in the summer months everyone went swimming anyway. Naturally one could envisage times when a bath would be appreciated, but these did not seem sufficiently frequent to justify occupying such a large space.

"If we took away the bathroom the saloon would be half again as big," pointed out Jess.

I was a little hesitant to embark on such an apparently destructive scheme, but finally agreed. We spent a busy afternoon tearing down the bathroom walls — and an even busier time manoeuvring the heavy cast iron bath out of the cabin and up the narrow stairs to the wheelhouse. At one time there were five of us trapped in a seemingly impossible position half way up the stairs, but somehow in the end brute strength triumphed.

Now we entered what afterwards we termed our plumbing phase. To remove the bath and washbasin we had, of course, first to seal off the water connections. This meant taking up the floor boards as a result of which, apart from having a somewhat alarming view of the very bowels of *Sanu*, we were confronted by lengths of rubber piping running here, there and everywhere.

Gradually we managed to identify the various pipes, and cut off the important ones. Next we had decided in place of the bathroom to put a small sink in each of the three cabins. This seemed a simple enough operation involving merely the running of supply and waste pipes to each room, where we fitted in three small sinks bought in readiness. We joined the various pipelines with jubilee clips, connected up the water — and turned on the taps.

"Stop it!" we cried simultaneously. "Shut off the water."

Water was squirting out from almost every join we had made . . . and now we learned a lesson of plumbing seared for ever into our minds. Check and double check and treble check every join — and then add putty! We found we had to start again from scratch, insert washers of squares of linoleum and tighten everything twice as tight as before — until at last we had the supply position in order. Then we had the same trouble over the waste pipes. Altogether I estimated we must have spent perhaps thirty hours over a job which probably an experienced plumber would have managed in three.

"Never mind," said Jess wearily. "It's one way of getting to know our boat."

Gradually, over the winter months, I began to realise how true this was. Through tackling various jobs ourselves, willy nilly we became more knowledgeable about the intricate working of *Sanu*. Soon we had ripped up the linoleum in the saloon, alarmed to find the boards beneath dripping wet from the condensation – it was a pleasure to see them dry out and then coat them with varnish. As far as possible we let the air get to every part of *Sanu*: meantime Jess and Gill were busy making fresh apricot-coloured hessian covers for the foam rubber seats in the saloon, which of course we had now extended to cover the area which had been the bathroom.

When all was finished we put down some plain Chinese matting, and felt reasonably pleased with our efforts. We had moved the diesel drip-through stove to one side, so that now we had a long L-shaped saloon big enough for a dozen people to relax in, in comfort. It was true, of course, that – mesmerised by the idea of expansion – I was beginning to suggest pulling down the double cabin and making the saloon even bigger, but Jess managed to restrain me. Instead we painted out the two front cabins, stripped the main beams of the saloon, painted the wheel-house again – and as a final domestic touch converted the two single bunks of our deck cabin into a more friendly double bed.

While busy with our interior decorating of *Sanu* I had not been forgetting the far more important matter of our engine – or perhaps I should begin to say, engines. From the moment we had first bought *Sanu* we had always felt slightly uneasy about the fact that she only had the single, though admittedly powerful, Kelvin diesel. Apparently it is quite the custom up in Scotland for fishing boats to have only the single engine, and that should be recommendation enough, for there are no better boats and, potentially, no worse conditions for boating. On the other hand, I well knew that this was not by any means the custom in the West Country; where most of the larger fishing boats have two engines (our contemporary, *Karenza*, at Newlyn, had a main and a wing engine).

When I discussed the problem once with David Saquie he made an expressive gesture. "Don't worry. It's a magnificent engine, it'll get you home on one cylinder if necessary." While first-hand experience had given me more and more confidence in our Kelvin, I could never rid myself of the unanswerable query — an engine *can* fail for a dozen reasons, and just *suppose* our engine did fail in circumstances where there was precious little time to do much about it? Supposing we were close to a rocky shore, with the tide carrying us in? We had no sails, and even if we had there might be no guarantee that they could get us out of such trouble. If, on the other hand, we had a second engine, even quite a small one, its presence might literally mean the difference between safety and disaster — even between life and death.

So, after a lot of humming and hawing, we had decided to order a second engine. Because we wanted an engine that was as uncomplicated as possible we chose an air-cooled type: a diesel of course, since these were obviously safest and most economical; and hand-starting to avoid any undue dependence on an electrical system. It was quite an education studying all the different catalogues and advertisements. For a time we toyed with the gamble of picking up a cheap second-hand engine, but in the end we felt that since this was a safety measure it was wisest to start from scratch and have a new engine. Finally we plumped for a 36-horse-power Lister and put an order through to the manufacturers in Gloucestershire. Mike Peters, a St. Ives marine engineer, agreed to handle the installation, with the help of his friend, Dick Pollard a shipwright, and before Christmas came they had cleared away some of the ballast on the port side of *Sanu* and bored a hole through the beams ready for the stern-tube and shaft. These were ordered from a firm in Scotland, and were expected within a week or two. It was the engine, actually, that we were worried about: there was a ten-week waiting period, as we understood, and that meant waiting nearly until Easter. As it happened, we were lucky : word came through within two weeks that there was an engine ready, and rather than lose the opportunity Mike Peters drove up to Gloucester and collected it in his van. . . . The next morning he called me round to his workshop, and there was the gleaming bright, gleaming new engine.

"We shan't be long now," he said cheerfully. "Soon as the stern tube comes we can get on with the job."

That was at the beginning of January. A week went by; another week; and yet another week. I began to get anxious, and persuaded Mike Peters to ring up Glasgow. The answer was elaborate and apologetic, but the gist of it was that so far nothing had been sent. Another week passed . . . and another. Now we were into February, and still no sign. More phone calls, more explanations. At one stage Mike Peters begged them to send just the tube, the rest later. . . . It seemed to make no difference. Another week of silence — AND ONE MORE WEEK! At long last he came and phoned up for the sixth time from our house and both of us heard a solemn pledge from the other end that the goods were on the way by passenger train. And in fact at the very end of that week, on a Friday afternoon, the stern tube finally arrived . . . just as Dick Pollard was due to start a two-week job that would prevent him doing any work for us! However, later that evening he and Mike Peters managed to get the stern tube installed, so that the shaft could be ordered, and the work was planned to be completed in a fortnight's time.

While waiting for the long-delayed stern tube I decided we might as well go ahead with a general check-up of our Kelvin engine. Like most of the big diesel engine makers, Kelvin's have a special service engineer for each district, and ours was the firm of Cowls, over at Porthleven. One crisp February day their chief engineer, Billy, drove over and I spent a couple of hours with him going through the engine's performance. I remembered that Doug had thought there was a bad lack of compression suggesting a

E*

worn piston or rings. So now when Billy nodded confirmation, I did not worry unduly, for I expected *some* repair work.

"Since I've got to take off that one," he said, "would you like me to check on them all? It's up to you."

At first I was tempted to leave well alone, since the old Kelvin seemed to be functioning quite well. However, this wasn't like a car—it was a hundred times more important to avoid a mechanical breakdown with a boat than a car, which can just be taken to the nearest garage.

"Very well—go ahead."

It was arranged that I should call back at the boat on the following afternoon to hear the verdict. At that time my mind was fairly preoccupied with other things, and anyway I had no particular reason to be apprehensive. Alas, I had hardly got down the ladder into the engine-room before one look at Billy's face struck a chill into my heart.

"Is it bad, then?"

It was; pretty well as bad as could be. Not only would he have to replace piston and liner on No. 3 chamber, but in fact the other liners were worn—and worse, much, much worse, when he came to examine the cylinder heads, three of them had hairline cracks in them, which meant water was getting past.

Furtively I sorted out the Kelvin spares list and began looking up prices. One look was enough to make me groan: cylinder heads were £20 each, and this price list was five years old.

"Prices are up 10 per cent. on that," said Billy apologetically.

Patently, there was nothing much else that could be done, but agree to the necessary work. There then began a curiously distasteful process of disembowelment—at one stage I came into the engine-room and it was rather like interrupting an operation at its most critical stage. Bits and pieces of my beloved Kelvin lay strewn all over the engine room . . . and in the centre, where usually that shining brass-topped engine stood so proudly, there was only a broken shell. I could hardly believe my eyes—and I could certainly not believe that Humpty Dumpty would ever be put together again.

But he was. Billy was one of those born mechanics who have grown into their vocations; somehow his thick oily fingers worked with all the skill of a surgeon, above all he was patient, extracting piece after piece. It was no joke either, sometimes, for certain parts of the Kelvin weighed more than one man could carry, and we had to use a truck to wheel them away to Billy's van. However, somehow it was all managed, and after only a week or so, I came down the ladder one Friday midday to find Billy smiling quietly to himself — and the engine, fully restored to health, humming away.

"I've had her running for two hours, she's fine now."

To demonstrate his confidence, Billy opened up the throttle, then turned her down, and our Kelvin — perhaps I should say our *new* Kelvin — first roared, and then murmured quietly.

Well, I thought, if it were done, 'twere better done well. . . .

While all this disembowelling of the Kelvin had been going on matters were still stagnant as far as the Lister was concerned. However, Jess and I had made a determined onslaught on the last remaining problem, the stripping down of the above-water part of *Sanu*'s hull, preparatory to a complete repainting. I am afraid I had been tempted to slap on a coat of paint, like most of the fishermen do each spring, but Jess was determined that we should make a fresh start altogether. This meant buying a Calor gas torch burner and tank, and laboriously burning away the paint — not, as one might have expected, one or even two coats, but four or five. In fact the work proved so arduous and lengthy that we were forced to call in some help from a friend of ours, Patrick, and soon life settled into quite a regular routine — Patrick would work alone all morning, and then each afternoon Jess and I would join him, and the three of us combine forces. We were very fortunate in the weather, for there was no rain, though plenty of cold winds. Gradually the bare wood of *Sanu* began to emerge, probably for the first time for twenty years . . . though only briefly, for as soon as we had stripped a section, at once we quickly brushed on a coat of grey primer to protect the wood. The next day we would put on one coat of undercoat, then another—until finally the whole boat, or rather all of it except one patch against the quay, was ready for the final gloss coat. For this we mixed up a pleasing powder-blue mixture, and finally one sunny Sunday at the beginning of March, with as many members of the family as could be mustered, we set about painting the gloss coat. There was Stephen on one ladder at one end, Jess on another near him, our son-in-law Alan on another ladder in the middle, and Gill and myself on the ground doing the lower levels. It was a combined operation that had to go off at high speed, for the tide was beginning to creep in—and indeed Stephen and Alan had to finish off their parts with the bottom of their ladders in two or three feet of water. . . . Inevitably there was trouble—Alan's rope gave way and he fell into the water—but fortunately only up to the waist.

At last the job was finished, even to the intricate design of the name plate on either side of the bow, which Alan had touched up in black on the white background. We all went on the quay and stood looking proudly down at a graceful blue and white elegant M.F.V., looking quite fresh and new. Then, as a final touch, we quickly painted up our main dinghy, and labelled her proudly: *Tender to Sanu*.

At last the time arrived for the delivery to our boat of the new second engine. When Mike Peters told me it would be necessary for us to take *Sanu* over from Lelant Wharf to Hayle quay I began to feel uneasy. It was nearly six months since I had taken *Sanu* anywhere, and I was not really familiar with the intricacies of Hayle estuary. Above all, I didn't want to make a poor showing, seamanship-wise, before local experts.

"For goodness sake," said Jess, as I lay in bed brooding, "it's only a few hundred yards. What can possibly go wrong?"

These are famous last words, etched into my unconscious for ever.

When the afternoon came, Mike drove round to Hayle with the new engine ready to be loaded on one of the huge cranes there — while Jess and I and Stephen and Dick prepared to go over the water way.

It was a lovely sunny spring afternoon, the tide had come in fast, it was time to go. Nervously I rushed about making sure all was well — then I went below and managed to start our diesel engine without too much fuss. On deck Dick was being rather officious about ropes and going astern before we swung her round and so on . . . but I knew that his was the voice of experience and obeyed implicitly. In fact we made quite a smart get away, steamed a hundred yards down, swung neatly round the fork in the estuary, and headed down the other stream towards the big communal quay where Mike waited with the engine.

Within a short time the 11-cwt. engine had been neatly dropped on deck, Mike joined us aboard, and off we set.

"Aim for that white post, and then bring her round," said Dick.

Feeling a growing air of confidence — even perhaps the beginnings of a pathetic secret dream that as a result of my competent handling of the boat that afternoon my status among the local fishermen would take a welcome uplift — I headed *Sanu* down by the white post. We were in rather confined waters indeed; a hundred yards away was the main quay, ahead of us a bank, to our starboard the warning posts of obstructions in the river. . . .

"Now bring her round. . . ."

I hauled on the wheel. *Sanu*'s bow began to swing round, until it was heading directly for the bank on the opposite side.

"Keep bringing her round . . ." said Dick. A few moments later: "Are you sure you're bringing her round?"

"I can't," I ejaculated in a frantic, strained voice. "There's something wrong." I hauled despairingly at a suddenly immovable wheel, tugging and tugging. Suddenly it wrenched itself out of my grasp and spun madly round.

"The steering's *jammed*!"

It was, too. . . . Leaving us with our bow headed for a sand-bank, our stern a few yards from the first of those dreaded wooden beacons, and our midships abreast of an incoming tide which would carry us very quickly upon a large quay wall.

For a moment I stood there petrified. Then Dick's calm voice sounded at my side.

"Put her into reverse. Give her a burst. Knock her out of gear."

By these processes, miraculously it seemed, our large boat was made to standstill in mid-water. The bank, the stakes, the wall — all remained fortunately at the same distance.

Meanwhile, we tore away the floor boards and examined the chain of the wheel, which seemed to have become locked below. Hammer! Spanner! Chisel! With them Mike poked and prodded while at the wheel I frantically carried out Dick's instructions.

"Now forward a bit . . . only a touch . . . knock her out . . . now into reverse . . . a bit of throttle, not too much . . . now knock her out."

As, like a marionette, I carried out these expert instructions, a part of me managed to take in the scene. Over on the quay the men were all watching . . . nearer at hand some interested spectators were gathering on the bank . . . meantime in a narrow area of water, in the heart of Hayle, our boat was helplessly going round and round, liable at any moment to hit a sandbank, perhaps even a rock. Indeed it was not impossible for *Sanu* actually to sink up the estuary, a mile from the sea. What a disaster! What ignominy! How would we ever face anyone again?

"Reverse . . . knock her out . . . forward. . . ."

Relentlessly we drifted towards the wall. Then at the last minute there was a shout of triumph from Mike as he loosened the chain, and the wheel spun free.

"Righto, Cap'n — away she goes."

Temporarily back in control, if it could be called that. I sent *Sanu* forward, away from those horrid walls and stakes. Soon we came to the fork in the estuary again, and it was necessary once more to make a sweeping turn. We managed somehow to negotiate the bend safely, but as we came down to our own quay again we were faced with the need to make yet another sharp turn against the strong tide. Praying devoutly, I swung the wheel hard over. . . . Prayers were not enough. There was an alarming tightening of the wheel, and all at once it became immovable.

"It's jammed again!" I cried in anguish.

This time we were even more vulnerable, broadside against a stream that would soon carry us on to a weir, with no control on the steering.

I stood there gripping the wheel forlornly. Everything was against me, we were doomed.

"Put her into reverse . . . knock her out . . . now forward . . . knock her out . . . into reverse."

Once more the quiet, knowledgeable voice came to my reason. We lumbered backwards and forwards, while Mike struggled again with the steering. Once again disaster loomed nearer and nearer, and once again at the last minute the steering was freed and we limped up against the quay . . . home at last, but somewhat shaken.

After all that trouble, the new engine still had to be manoeuvred laboriously down into the aft cabin and then into the main engine-room, where Dick had cleared space for it and made a solid wooden bed. There was a lot more complicated work fitting air ducts and extending controls to the wheelhouse, but at long last, only a week or so before our winter sojourn would be ended, the second engine was finally installed and tested. It took up quite a lot of room and had cost a lot of money we could ill afford, but at least we could go to sea knowing that if anything ever did go wrong with our main engine, we were not in any danger of drifting to disaster.

And now, spring was in the air, even summertime had been brought in, during a March which had in fact begun with snow-storms and blizzards. Our winter hibernation was nearly ended. Now in the last week or so we rushed round finishing off at lot of last-minute jobs, and more especially giving a last coat of gloss paint to one side of the boat which we had not been able to get at before. Our final task was to give the entire deck a final coat of red Dekaplex, hoping that, apart from the aesthetic effect, it might stop some of the odd leaks that were still bothering us.

At last one sunny afternoon we stood on the quay at Lelant looking down on what might well have been a new boat alto-gether. Gone were the rather drab black and faded green colours — here was a bright shining blue and white fishing vessel, as cheerful as any of the French boats. Somehow the use of the powder blue seemed to have emphasised the beauty of *Sanu*'s portly curves . . . she looked, we felt proudly, quite the belle of the estuary. And eager, as we were now, to be out and about.

10

April in Paris

It seemed only fitting that we should mark the anniversary of our acquiring *Sanu*, and also the beginning of our first full new season, by making our most ambitious voyage – more than 1,000 miles in all. During those long winter months, when we weren't rushing backwards and forwards to work on the boat at Lelant Quay, we spent many exciting evenings pouring over maps and charts. By now, in my first rush of enthusiasm, I had acquired rather an embarrassing collection, including some for the Baltic Sea and others for Portugal! However, we realised that, if only for reasons of time limitations, we had better restrict ourselves from such ventures at the moment. Our Easter Cruise, as it became known, would have to be confined to the period of the school holidays, about three weeks. Where then to go? Ireland, Scotland? Brittany? Holland? There seemed quite a choice, but before long I found my mind fixing pretty clearly on travelling by sea and then up the River Seine into the heart of Paris. It was a journey that seemed to me to offer a little bit of everything: a sea crossing, visits to large ports like Cherbourg, the interest of a famous river like the Seine, and the final novelty of mooring our boat right in the centre of one of the world's most beautiful cities. I must also confess that, as one who prefers calm waters, the fact that more than half of our trip would be made in the comparative peace of an inland waterway did have a certain influence.

Once again I judged it wise to embark on the most meticulous preplanning, and letters began to flow backwards and forwards.

First I wrote to the French firm who published detailed charts of the River Seine, then to the French Touring Office, who supplied masses of useful booklets, then to the Seine Navigation authorities from whom I had to obtain a special permit—next, on a more individual plane, there were letters to such people as the secretaries of the Yacht Club of Cherbourg and of Le Havre, both of whom assured me it would be convenient to moor my 60-ft. boat off their clubs—and yet another letter to the director of Dubigeon-Normandie, a big boatyard at Rouen, who undertook to lower our masts for us (for once past Rouen there are innumerable low bridges across the Seine). This business of exact measurements began to dominate my thoughts for quite a time, and I was endlessly climbing about *Sanu* with a tape measure. In the end we learned that the maximum measurements of a boat travelling up the Seine to Paris were: length 426 ft. 2 in., beam 38 ft., draught 9 ft. 10 in., height above waterline, 16 ft. 5 in. Obviously we were all right for length and beam, but on draught we only had two feet to spare, and the height of our wheel-house was a good fourteen feet, which meant we were going to have a tight squeeze through some of the bridges. We would have very much liked to have been able to make a complete trip right across France to the Mediterranean, but we now found, as we had been told before, that *Sanu*'s beam and draft made this impossible—indeed, we could not even go beyond Paris.

Ah, well, at least we could go to Paris. As the winter months slowly passed, and we survived all our endless problems over the old and new engines, we kept telling ourselves, never mind, there's something to look forward to. And indeed there was no doubt that while a few of our ultra-cautious friends looked on us as crazy, most people envied us very much the opportunity—particularly our children's friends who obviously longed to come with us. Alas, we just had not the room, nor could take on the responsibility for such a long trip. As it was, at one time we were committed to taking about thirteen people, but in the end two couples dropped out, and the final crew consisted of nine — myself and Jess, Martin and Stephen, Demelza and Genevieve, a young honeymoon couple, Mike and Maureen Richards, and a friend Greta Perry, who volunteered to take on the onerous post of "galley slave". This was the idea of Jess whose enthusiasm for the trip waned at the thought of having to cook endless meals for nine people : the arrangement of actually employing someone to take on that daily task made an enormous difference, and we were able really to relax from all chores.

When April finally arrived we seemed to be engulfed by the preparations. There was tinned food supplies to be installed, including such items as coffee and tea, which we knew to be either short or very expensive in France. Soon *Sanu*'s galley began to look like a shop counter and we wondered if we had overdone things (but in retrospect were rather sorry we had not laid in still more, for prices were to prove exorbitant). Blankets, pillows, sleeping bags, tea cloths, towels, soap . . . fuel for the main engine, fuel for the second engine, reserve supplies of oil. Things were run so close that we did not actually test out our new engine until the day before we were due to leave St. Ives.

At last, however, it was midday on the Saturday, and we all assembled for a last drink at the "Sloop", on the waterfront at St. Ives. It was a tantalising sort of day : the sun shone, the sky was blue — but the sea was badly ruffled, and round on the Porthmeor side, definitely disturbed. As we toasted the success of our voyage we were beset with advice from the local fishermen — some saying, "Don't go" — others, knowing our sturdy boat, saying' "Yes, you'll be all right." In the end, after ringing up the coastguards at St. Just and making sure there was nothing really dangerous on the way, I decided we should make a start. After all, the first leg of the journey from St. Ives to Newlyn was the shortest of the whole trip.

Yes, but . . .! In fact it proved to be far and away the roughest, as well. From the moment we left St. Ives the boat was pitching and rolling and when we got down by Pendeen and rounded Cape Cornwall towards Land's End, we were having to take the sea on our beam, which was not at all comfortable. Several of Stephen's school friends had begged to come on this part of the trip round to Newlyn, and I think they began to be rather sorry!

It was just as we were passing the Longships lighthouse that the unbelievable happened: there was a sudden ominous silence. We looked at one another in consternation. "The engine's stopped!" Within seconds Mike and I had raced down into the engine-room, where we found a scene of minor chaos. The beam seas had been so rough that they had dislodged a 100-gallon water tank, which had in turn knocked a hefty oil drum against the engine—and by an almost incredible bit of bad luck the impact had turned off the tap of the fuel pipe! At such a moment, knowing we were literally only about a hundred yards off the Longships, there was no time to be wasted priming and starting the big engine. Mike and I turned thankfully to our new Lister, he swung with all his might and I pulled over the lever—and, thank goodness, the engine roared into life. Martin at the wheel in the deckhouse was able to steer *Sanu* away from the coast, very slowly of course, while Mike and I turned to the big engine. The trouble was that coming down into the fumes of the engine-room was not inducive to a state of peace: before long I had to give way to the inevitable bout of sea-sickness—only the second time I had ever been sick on *Sanu*, and, as on the previous occasion, on the first trip of the season. However, after recovering, I took turns with Mike at swinging and soon we had the Kelvin roaring into life. Ironically enough, from that moment to the end of the trip three weeks later we never had a moment's worry again from the main engine.

We were certainly glad to get into Newlyn that evening, but soon recovered our spirits with a tot of spirits all round and a big meal. We went to bed early, for we planned to be off at six in the morning—and so we were. The reason for the early start was that we wanted to go into Salcombe for that evening, and there is a sand bar across Salcombe; with high tide at about three, it was imperative that we reached there not much later than four-thirty. Thanks to the extra power of our second engine, which we now had on all the time as well as the main one, we made an excellent run to Salcombe, and though there was quite a swell across the entrance, my familiarity from previous visits made the entry quite straightforward. Not so the problem of anchoring, however. On previous visits we had just dropped our anchor opposite the Marine Hotel and that had been that. On this afternoon there was a very strong wind blowing down the estuary, as well as a heavy swell, and twice we dropped anchor and found it dragging. In the end we managed to get a hold, but just to be on the safe side put out a second anchor.

That evening we had our first real sample of Greta's cooking, and very tasty it was too. We were just sitting back replete afterwards when Martin, who had gone up on deck for a moment shouted down: "The dinghy's gone!" We had lowered the big dinghy and left it tied up at the stern – now we found that under the combined strength of wind and swell she had frayed her mooring rope and disappeared into the night. This was a blow, indeed, for though we had with us a small Mirror dinghy belonging to Stephen, we relied on the large dinghy for most of our trips ashore. It was dark outside, but we knew that below the ship there were two creeks, and that the dinghy must have floated down and gone ashore somewhere. Mike and Stephen bravely decided to investigate in the small dinghy, and after reluctantly donning life-belts, for it was quite nasty out there with the swell, they disappeared into the darkness . . . to return an hour later, covered in mud, with no good news to report.

There was nothing left but to sleep on it. Fortunately the next morning there was a chugging noise and the Salcombe harbour-master came alongside us in his launch, accompanied by a familiar figure in the form of Geoff Scott, who had helped us bring *Sanu* down from Southampton a year ago. They took Mike and Stephen

off in tow for a tour of inspection, and later that morning we
witnessed a triumphal return procession – the harbour-master's
launch towing Mike and Stephen in their dinghy, in turn towing
our large white dinghy, looking rather the worse for wear, mud-
wise, but intact, even including its engine. This was a great relief,
which we celebrated that evening with a drink with Geoff in the
King's Arms at Salcombe. Ironically enough, that very afternoon
I was sitting on the deck of *Sanu* sunning myself when to my
astonishment I saw a small boat floating past. I grabbed a boat-
hook and managed to catch it. Someone else had lost a dinghy in
much the same way as ourselves, so we were able to do a good
turn to balance our own reward.

Not only because of losing the dinghy, but owing to a bad
weather forecast, we had to spend a day weather-bound in Salcombe. The next forecast was more cheerful, and at seven o'clock
in the morning we raised our anchors and crept out of Salcombe
and set out across the Channel bound for Cherbourg. We had
worked out a course which should bring us on to Cap Hague, and
the boat fairly raced along, with a wind behind it. When at last
we spied land we felt rather pleased with ourselves. Then something about the shape began to worry me, and I turned to my
invaluable Adlard Cole book, with its photographs of important
landmarks. Yes, there could be no doubt – that was not Cap
Hague, it was the Casquets, and we were two or three degrees off
course. It was nothing serious; we just altered course slightly and
headed on past Alderney and towards Cap Hague, which we
could now see ahead. By seven o'clock that evening we had passed
on down the French coast and were approaching the big breakwater at Cherbourg, with its convenient landmark of Port d'Est.
The entry proved quite simple, what with our course already
plotted and Adlard Cole's meticulous series of photographs, and
soon we had crossed Petit Rade and found our way to the inner
harbour. Here, of course, following extensive correspondence, I
fully expected to find someone from the Cherbourg Yacht Club

on hand, at least to take a rope. We saw the lines of yachts moored, and edged in, but there was no sign of anyone expecting us, so in the end we made for a long quay beyond, and tied up there for the night. I jumped ashore and ran down to the Yacht Club, a modern and impressive building, to find it all shuttered up and a large sign FERMEZ – apparently closed for a two-day holiday. Not really downhearted, for we had found a mooring, anyway, we went back to the boat and sat down patiently to await the Customs men, for whose benefit we were dutifully flying a yellow flag. Back home the customs are aboard almost before you have tied up a rope, but here it became obvious things were different. Nobody was interested. After waiting an hour, we shrugged and gave up, and then we all went ashore to have our first French meal in a Cherbourg restaurant. We were delighted with the swift and efficient service and the tasty dishes, especially the way a succulent soup was brought in a tureen and left for second helpings, but somewhat alarmed by a bill of nearly £10. This was our first experience of a problem that was to haunt us for most of the trip. Prices in France seemed very, very high: meat, butter, poultry, even cheese and vegetables and fruit – all cost at least twice as much as in England. Bread and milk were more reasonable, but there was really only one item which offered a real saving, *le Vino*. How we enjoyed really being able to indulge ourselves, sampling lovely cool bottles of Anjou Rosé or Sylvaner, all at about a quarter of their cost in Britain.

When we returned to *Sanu* for the night we had recovered from the shock of the restaurant bill and all slept very well – to be awoken soon after dawn by bangings on the wheel-house door. Outside stood several gesticulating fishermen. It appeared we were occupying their traditional berths at the quay and must move at once, so we started up the engine and moved over to a large buoy in the centre of the harbour. Just as we were relaxing again a big launch purred up and a handsome young customs official came aboard looking rather important and demanding to see our docu-

ments. At first he was a little grim and stiff, but as soon as his appreciative eye fell upon our pretty young honeymooner, Maureen, relations seemed to improve greatly. In fact the examination was perfunctory; after sampling the prices in France we realised that they were hardly likely to be much worried about anything coming in from their poor cousin, Britain.

After a day in Cherbourg we headed off down the French coast for Le Havre, a straightforward trip provided we managed to find, at the end of it, the Le Havre light vessel. It wasn't all that easy, but it helped to know that about every other boat in the vicinity would be heading in much the same direction. From the light vessel we altered course for Le Havre itself, quite a tricky approach between two lines of buoys. Once again we had made excellent progress, about seventy miles in eight hours, and after rounding the Digue du Nord we were pleasantly surprised to find a large buoy awaiting just as we had been told by letter. We tied up and looked forward, after a meal, to going ashore by dinghy to explore Le Havre – alas, there was such a big swell coming into the harbour, and we were so exposed to it that it would have been impossible to go ashore without a great deal of discomfort and inconvenience. So we left it and had an early night, ready for an equally early start in the morning.

At seven we were ready to make our historic entrance into the River Seine, but there were so many large liners queuing up to enter Le Havre that we had to wait our chance for nipping out. Then, when we found the buoys marking the entry to the river, we were a little alarmed to discover thick mist forming ahead. I had read that mist was the principal hazard on the Seine and now understood why: it was rather alarming suddenly to find a huge tanker looming out upon us. Fortunately as the morning passed the mist dispersed, and soon we were able to relax. I must say we were all most impressed with the amount of traffic carried on the Seine – we have no river in Britain to compare, from the commercial point of view.

Our second favourable impression was the river itself and its lovely background. How pleasant, after huge vistas of open sea to see the meandering green hills and wooded valleys, and every now and then a typical riverside town, seeming almost to grow round the water. We stayed our first night at one of these, Duclair, moored up to one of several landing stages. Here we discovered one of the French co-operatives, where prices, particularly of wines, were lower than anywhere else. Despite our linguistic limitations we found no difficulties — there was always pen and paper to work out the prices. In the evening Jess and I and Mike and Maureen escaped for a pleasant drinking session in a riverside café where, under the influence of the local *vino*, we decided gaily that this was the life, this was.

The next morning, starting off in excellent humour, we found after going a mile or two that the new small engine had failed — and that at the same time our bilge pumps had become blocked. We managed to fix the engine but could not at first get the bilges to work — so there was nothing for it but to get the whole ship's company to muster on deck and start operating the four hand-pumps, a truly wearisome task, since each one required about 600 pumps.

At the end we walked about with aching muscles. After that Stephen and I vowed we couldn't face it again so we went down into the engine-room and took the bilge pumps to pieces, clearing the pipes and then nervously screwing everything back in place. To our joy, they worked at once.

Another setback awaited us at Rouen, where we had arranged to have our masts lowered. When we pulled into the Dubigen-Normandie boatyard we became alarmed to see large signs of in-activity. When I went to investigate I found that the whole yard was closed down for a four-day Easter holiday. There was nothing for it but a do-it-yourself effort. Michael, who was used to working on fishing boats, worked out a plausible if rather hazardous method of using ropes tied round our anchor winch and gingerly we managed to lower each mast in turn and then get them tied up on our wheel house roof.

Feeling rather pleased with ourselves we set off now through the port of Rouen — which might well have been Southampton, judging by the huge ships lined up, whereas in fact it was seventy miles inland. After a while the big ships were left behind as we began passing under long low bridges, and soon we were out of Rouen and heading up river. All at once the nautical environment changed: there were no more huge liners, but in their place literally dozens and dozens of long low steel barges, used for carrying cargoes not only up to Paris but on and through waterways all over France. Each seemed to be operated by a couple and their family — many of them had long lines of washing drying on the decks, and children running around. Most of these barges were twice as long as our own boat and when, as often was the case, they were lashed together in fours or sixes, pushed by a tug, they made a formidable sight. When loaded they would sink so low in the water that it was quite easy to miss seeing them. Altogether I found navigation on the Seine was far trickier than I had imagined, and was very glad of my detailed charts. On the other hand the French waterways arrangements seem very thorough; the most detailed systems were worked out, so that boats going one way went under one arch of a bridge, and boats coming down under another. We never had any real trouble, and found the barge skippers a friendly lot, usually exchanging waves as we passed. Perhaps because it was early in the season we were actually the only pleasure boat seen on the river either going to Paris or returning.

That night we reached our first lock, at Amfreville de Poses, and tied up by a barge. The next day, Easter Sunday, we set off early hoping perhaps to reach Paris. We were now passing through beautiful stretches of countryside, with great châteaux perched on the top of hills and vast stretches of green fields. We travelled about twenty-five miles to the next lock — and then found it was

closed for the day. There was nothing for it but to pull in and tie
up to a single barge that was moored by the river bank. We came
alongside carefully and Stephen jumped aboard the barge to tie a
rope. A few moments later I found two sad-looking figures gesticulating from the barge wheel-house, the woman pointing . . .
at the remains of a milk pudding she had put out to cool, and upon
which Stephen had firmly stepped. We hastily sent over a tin of
fruit as a peace offering, and in fact, despite the unfortunate
introduction, we soon made friends. They were charming people,
a couple who talked to us about their life taking loads up and
down the French waterways: mostly their cargo seemed to con-
sist of oats and barley, for export to English whisky makers!

At one stage the skipper took us down into his engine room. It
was spotlessly clean, putting ours to shame—there was even a big
panel with a slot for every single tool in the right place, which I
eyed with envy thinking of our regrettable habit of removing
tools and forgetting to return them. Unlike our cumbersome hand-
starting of the Kelvin, the barge skipper had an air-starting
system; just a flick and a twirl, and she was purring away. The
domestic quarters were quite large, too, and obviously their life
was quite a comfortable one.

To pass the time we all went for a long walk in the picturesque
Normandy countryside. It appeared a well-to-do area, and we kept
coming upon one huge villa after another, many of them obviously used as week-end retreats. Everywhere there were tables and
chairs in the gardens and people relaxing in the sudden sunshine.
We walked on, and Maureen picked a large bunch of wild may
blossom. As we returned the barge skipper's wife smiled and said
rather sweetly, "Ah, we call those the flowers of love."

Easter Monday was the day we had planned to reach Paris, and
we made a very great effort, starting at seven in the morning and
covering 100 miles by dusk. This entailed passing through several
of the huge French locks, most of which have three chambers, and
house half a dozen enormous barges at a time. I must admit I felt

nervous for *Sanu*'s safety, crammed between the slimy lock walls and a huge steel barge, but we survived. On and on we pounded, not only with both main and second engine going, but also with our generator humming away, for we found on such a voyage, with long evenings in the saloon, we used up electricity at an alarming rate. When we passed through the lock at Bougail, some forty-five kilometres from Paris, at about six we thought perhaps we might reach our destination, but in the end we reached the last lock at Suresnes just too late, to find everything shut up. We had to pass an impatient night there, one that was greatly relieved by a truly magnificent spaghetti dish made by our ever-improving chef. At first, I think she felt overwhelmed, but later became very efficient at whipping up meals for nine and even at one period eleven.

All the way up the Seine the weather had not been too kind, and now, as if determined to serve up a spectacular finale, it worsened. When, early the next morning, we took our place in the Suresnes lock for the last passage it was already raining heavily. Afterwards, as we began passing Bois de Boulogne and there ahead of us saw the famed shape of the Eiffel Tower — now, of all times, the rain turned to sleet, and as at last we approached Pont Alexandre and headed for the Touring Club de France, it was actually snowing.

Fortunately when nine people have survived crossing the English Channel and several more days at sea and journeying up river in a comparatively small boat, their spirits are not going to be dampened by rain or snow. There was a slight pause as somewhat astonished officials of the Touring Club of France held a debate about what to do with our rather bulky *Sanu*, then they finally found us a perfect berth at the quayside. By midday on our first morning we had all taken advantage of the excellent shower facilities provided, and emerged sartorially splendrous, ready to see the sights.

Our position at the Port de Plaisance, close to the Quai D'Orsay, was pretty convenient all round: a short stroll brought us to

Champs-Elysées and bus and metro soon took us farther afield. There were often times when Jess and I wished that we were on our own, to be really free to wander at will and enjoy the numerous wonders of Paris. On the other hand, we were pleased to find that the children really did enjoy the novelty of the experience. In particular we were interested at their reaction when taken into the big art galleries like the Louvre — they were constantly tugging at our sleeves and demanding that we came to see the Mona Lisa or some other famous picture, which to them had previously been just a name in a book. I think we were all most thrilled by a visit to the main Impressionist exhibition, in a wing of the Louvre. It was a truly sensual pleasure to walk up a staircase and see a grand vista of Van Goghs or the wondrous hazy landscapes of Monet or the lovely Renoir and Degas nudes — all on their original canvases.

Another memorable occasion was when I piloted our large party out to a Montparnasse cinema to see a performance of Jacques Tatti in *Jour de Fete*. We were unprepared for the gaiety with which the cinema staff had planned the evening. Not only was the cinema foyer specially decorated, but before the main film there was a sudden burst of music and in marched a brass band, obviously based on the one in the film, to entertain us for half an hour . . . and when they left dozens of bright balloons were hurled down on the audience from the gallery by the attendants. Our English film shows are never such fun!

Our children had several outings of their own, including a visit to the Olympia to hear Les Kinks. Over in Britain, of course, such groups are very popular, with the result that many of our teenage boys have long hair, our son Stephen being no exception. In France, obviously, this is still a rarity, and in one restaurant the manager, with a mischievous smile, approached Stephen brandishing a large pair of scissors.

Most of our shopping for the boat, while in Paris, was done in Rue St. Dominique, just across the river, where we found prices more reasonable. We would have liked to eat out more, but funds simply would not permit; however, we did enjoy two special evenings. The first was for the whole company, nine of us along with two friends who were visiting us — we decided on this occasion to follow the advice of one of the tourist leaflets and visit one of those restaurants which offer a special tourist meal at a price of about 8 francs a head. By the time we had ordered half a dozen bottles of wine, of course, the cost had risen considerably, but we did feel we had value for money. This was the evening when, like proper tourists, we roamed about the brightly lit streets of Montmartre, and a goggle-eyed Stephen was enticed into one of the strip clubs by an apparent charge of only 2 francs 50 cents — soon to emerge very indignant at being asked 20 francs for a glass of orangeade! It was also the evening, regrettably, when our 13-year-old teenager, Demelza, partook of more rosé than was good for her, and on the way home, much to our embarrassment, kept declaring at the top of her young voice: "Down with de Gaulle!"

Our other evening was a more private one, just Jess and I and Mike and Maureen. We strolled past Notre Dame and found a delightful red-table-cloth restaurant by the edge of the river, where we wined and dined excellently, ending up dancing with the manager and other diners, to the strains of an Italian accordionist. Afterwards a taxi back to Port de Plaisance and then we all leaned over the bridge looking down on the waters of the Seine, now sparkling with reflected lights — and there, below us, the warm friendly glow of our own sturdy boat, *Sanu*. These are the moments one remembers dearly after voyaging abroad in your own boat.

Our trip back down the Seine was much quicker than the upward one, for of course we now had the current with us. Indeed, we travelled much of the way at the startling speed of twelve knots, passing most of the heavily laden barges. The sun was shining at long last and we were relaxing thinking to ourselves, we know the route, nothing much can go wrong. . . . At last as dusk approached we decided to pull in behind a row of barges waiting for the morning of the lock ahead. On this occasion Mike was at the wheel, so I went forward with a rope, ready to jump ashore. As *Sanu* glided in closer and closer to the bank I stood idly waiting, watching the rear of the steel barge coming nearer, and waiting for Mike to put the boat into reverse. I waited . . . and waited . . . and suddenly, with a terrifying movement, *Sanu* seemed to leap forward and went straight into the back of the barge! The moment is etched into my mind: I could not really believe my eyes. What had happened of course has happened to me – in a momentary confusion Mike put the gear into forward instead of reverse, and by the time he corrected the mistake it was too late.

The next few moments were rather comic. Apparently the crew of the barge must have been asleep, for there was silence for a few horrified moments, and then they came rushing on deck, gesticulating and making anguished movements of their hands. Mike and I stood there apologising profusely, and it did not help to discover they knew not a word of English. At last when they had calmed down the skipper demanded that we accompany him to make an official report. By now it was dark, and rather miserably Mike and I followed him along the tow path and across the lock chambers to the offices of the head lock-keeper. Here a real pantomime took place, with the lock-keeper and the skipper knowing no English, and Mike and I pretty ill-equipped with French. Between us we had to fill up about four official forms, including lengthy descriptions of our boat and what had happened. By the time it was all over Mike and I crawled back exhausted. Even then we had had to promise that one of us would be available at six in the morning for an official measurement of the damaged parts of the barge. Mike took on this task, and later when we came down for breakfast we found him rather dazed – apparently the occasion had been more token than important; afterwards they had all sat down and drank whisky together!

We were glad to press on the next day, and went as far down the river as Villequiex, not far from the estuary mouth. Here we

had an early night hoping to make a good start in the morning
. . . but awoke to find the boat completely shrouded in mist, with
traffic on the river at a standstill. It was very eerie and impossible,
and we were just resigning ourselves to spending the day there,
when, about ten o'clock, the mist quite abruptly cleared. I was
uneasy about making Cherbourg before dark with such a late start,
but we decided to try. We then set off on what was probably the
most wonderful day of the whole trip, gliding in brilliant sunshine to the mouth of the Seine and then on over a dead calm sea
to Cape Barfleur. Just in case we got caught out in the dark I had
swotted up the lights of the relevant buoys, and now I was glad
I had, for dusk quickly turned into dark. However, rounding the
Cape I was able to identify the first buoy, and then the second, and
headed for the third, beyond which Cherbourg lay only two miles
away — and then, somehow, I couldn't find it. Suddenly, what had
been all peaceful and pleasant, for me at any rate, turned into a
minor nightmare. My eyesight is not so good now, and we have a
rather weak light on our compass anyway, so that all at once I was
having to put on glasses to read the compass then take them off
again to look ahead at the bewildering vista of lights that indicated Cherbourg. Jess was with me for a time, but I was becoming
irritable now, and after a few exchanges she retired in high
dudgeon leaving me to bring *Sanu* into harbour in the dark on my
own — a state of responsibility which worried me still more. Martin
came up to keep me company and between us we tried to identify a
wandering winking red light and a green light in the right position, which would indicate the eastern approach to Cherbourg.
However, the nearer we got the less I liked the look of the surrounding vague shadowy shapes, that could well be that cursed
breakwater. . . . Finally I swung the boat away, thinking better
to be safe than sorry. At this stage Mike came up and kindly took
over the wheel while I retired to make an intensive study of our
charts for every scrap of information about the night entry into
Cherbourg. In the end, wisely as it happened, we decided to take a

F

bit longer and make for the western entrance, Fort d'Est, which was more easily identifiable by a winking light. At long last, with Mike confidently handling the wheel and more than atoning for his momentary lapse of a day ago, we crept into Cherbourg – two hours later than we should have been, but at least intact.

Our last morning was devoted to raising our masts again, then we pooled all our remaining francs and centimes and bought a last few bottles of wine. At two-thirty in the afternoon we set off homeward bound with both engines roaring away, steaming on and on down the English Channel right through the night – our second trip since acquiring the boat. They were not such pleasant conditions as the return from the Channel Islands, indeed it was Force 5–6 most of the way, but we made much quicker progress thanks to the other engine. Also this time we had the sense to organise a system of watches, so that two of us were on for three hours, and then off for six. Finally at about eight in the morning we sighted high land which we hoped was the Lizard, but proved to be cliffs more towards Falmouth. But at least we were not far off; five hours later we had rounded Land's End and were actually heading into St. Ives Bay – where we had to anchor for a couple of hours before being able to make our final landfall in the harbour. By that time the various coast-guards must have passed their message round, for, though I have never before seen a customs man at St. Ives, there was one waiting to jump aboard to check on us and our cargo. So ended a trip which none of us would have missed for the world, despite bad weather – and from which, parents and children alike, we learned more about our neighbour, France, than would have been possible through a more conventional form of travel.

11

Around the Western Isles

For our second major voyage in *Sanu* – indeed, far and away the longest and most ambitious of all our journeys – there was a certain amount of family disagreement. Jess, tired of English weather (but blessed by a blissful ignorance of the geographical facts of life) was all for a trip to sunny Spain. Since it seemed to me that this would involve a hazardous trip across the Bay of Biscay and perhaps a total outward journey of a thousand miles, I was not enthusiastic. Besides, I had already set my nautical sights firmly in a different direction – colder and less equable, perhaps, but offering exciting prospects of grandeur and native beauty. In the end the skipper's relentless persuasiveness won the day and it was agreed that the whole of the summer school holidays should be devoted to a voyage up the west coast of England and Wales and into the romantic sounding world of the Western Isles of Scotland, or the Hebrides.

As usual I embarked on my favourite practice of gathering in a complete list of charts – this time even I was somewhat dumbfounded to find that I had to spend nearly £15 on some thirty-five separate charts (subsequently I was to be eternally grateful for such foresight, as we headed *Sanu* nervously down intricate channels between fearsome rocks and reefs). I had never been to West Scotland before, but had it firmly fixed in my mind that such misty islands as Skye and Mull and Arran were "musts"; in addition, I had always had a yen to travel down the Caledonian Canal, which cuts Scotland in half, and also to visit the really, shorter Crinan Canal.

When finally, at eight o'clock on a late July evening, we embarked from St. Ives for Scotland, we were in the gayest of moods. All our plans had been completed satisfactorily, we were well stocked up with food and oil and water, and we were really looking forward to the complete change from a St. Ives overrun by trippers, to the solitary grandeur of the Highlands. We were to be much the same contingent as had made the trip to the Channel Isles – Jess and I, Martin and Stephen and Nicky, his friend, Demelza and Genevieve, Gill and her husband, Alan, Frank and Kate Baker and their daughter, Josephine – plus one very important addition, our tiniest passenger yet: Emily, our 3-month-old granddaughter of Gill and Alan. Frank and Kate and Josephine would be joining us at our first port of call, Fishguard. Meanwhile, the rest of us had a jolly parting drink at the "Sloop", on the harbour front at St. Ives, and it was in the cheeriest of moods that we walked along to set off. The forecast had been 3–4, which wasn't bad from our experience.

Forecast or no forecast, we had hardly left the shelter of St. Ives bay when *Sanu* began lurching about violently, rolling and tossing as if in the hands of demons – a mode of travel which was to persist right through the long, long night and until dawn, breaking somewhere near the Pembrokeshire coast, heralded a welcome calming down in the weather. We were all of us sick, some several times, and it was altogether a sorry beginning to our five-week voyage. We were thoroughly glad to reach Fishguard, there to be cheerfully welcomed by our friends, unsullied by the night's experience. Truth to tell, we felt rather like staying in the protection of Fishguard harbour, but pulling ourselves resolutely together, we set off early the next morning for Holyhead, and on to the Isle of Man.

Our experience of the latter place was pleasantly surprising – we had not expected much, but in fact found the interior country (seen rather delightfully on the little railway trip from Peel to Douglas) quite lovely, and comparatively unspoiled. Peel, which was the harbour we called at – and, because of bad weather, re-mained in for three days – was a cosy little town, dominated by the Manx kipper. We discovered that whereas in Cornwall the tourists send their friends packets of cream, from the Isle of Man it is the Manx kipper, and we sent off several.

When at last the weather improved and we were due to leave Peel, we experienced the first of several traumatic adventures which were to colour our Scottish trip. Our berth was well up the har-bour, and with several rows of Belfast fishing boats behind us the most obvious way of extricating ourselves was to turn round with-in the harbour. I knew there was a rather troublesome sand-bank somewhere in the centre and was careful to ask a fisherman if we had enough depth to turn across it. He – thinking, I since discovered, that we had as sharp a turning point as the Belfast boats – said we would manage it easily. In good faith, therefore, I took *Sanu* hard over to port and headed down the centre of the harbour . . . until suddenly the land on either side of us ceased to move by, and we realised we had run aground. What's more (and much worse) aground on a falling tide.

For five or ten minutes we ran both engines flat out, reversing and then changing forward, then back to reverse again – all with-out avail. Then much to our relief, there were some reassuring calls from among the Belfast men, and to our great relief we saw two of their hefty 60-ft. trawlers getting up steam and beginning to move out. Apparently it was a fairly common occurrence for boats to get caught on this sandbank, including the fishermen themselves, so they understood the predicament only too well. In no time at all they had manoeuvred near enough to take our ropes and with several sharp tugs – it was not by any means all that easy, with the tide falling rapidly – managed to haul us free.

Our troubles, however, were not over. After this rather shatter-ing experience, we put in to the outer end of the quay, partly to thank our rescuers, partly to fill up with water. As we came in, fortunately very slowly indeed, I had a strange impression that

when I put the boat into reverse, nothing really happened. However, we had got our ropes ashore by then and tied up, so I said
nothing until I had been over to thank the fishermen. When I came
back Stephen was shaking his head dolefully.

"The propeller wasn't going round when you reversed."

We stood staring unhappily into the green water, trying not to
credit this latest prospect of disaster. What could have happened?

At that very moment a couple more Belfast fishermen stepped
aboard with friendly grins. I can't possibly reproduce the Belfast
brogue, except to say that to us southerners it was almost incom-
prehensible. However, I gathered that they were saying they had
heard we might be having a bit of engine trouble, could they help?

"Well," I said dubiously, "our reverse seems a bit dicey."

It was more than that, as they speedily proved—it had packed
up. For a very simple reason—our shaft that runs from the engine
to the propeller is in two parts, joined by a coupling, and the rear
section had slipped out of the coupling.

On my own such an occurrence would have seemed the direct
disaster, since it posed a problem new to me and I really had no
idea what had to be done to repair matters. Not so our two Belfast
friends—they were very familiar with such an occurrence from
their own boats, and they knew exactly what had to be done. It
was a process of laborious work with mallet and crowbar and span-
ners that took about four or five hours, but at the end of it,
miraculously, our shafts were joined again—and this time, we
had a shrewd idea, more strongly than ever before. During the
whole time Stephen and I had watched with close interest, and we
had the added comfort that, if the same thing happened some
other time in the future, we now knew exactly what to do.

We insisted on paying the fishermen something for their
troubles, but we knew that this wasn't important—what was very
touching to us was the knowledge that these men just naturally
came to our aid out of good fellowship. This was a warming trait
we also found among the Scottish fishermen—ever ready to lend

a hand or give advice. This is probably a characteristic of fishermen everywhere, but nowhere have we found it more readily
evident than during our Scottish trip.

The next day the weather really cleared and we made a good trip
up to Stranraer and then on up the Firth of Clyde past Arran and
up Loch Fynne to the port of Tarbert. This was probably the
finest day of all our trip, the sun blazing down, the sea as calm as
the proverbial millpond – and all around us such fascinating sights
as Ailsa Craig, rising up in stark granite splendour in the middle
of nowhere, and then the wild grandeur of Arran and its Holy
Isle. There was literally not a tremor on the still waters, and the
entire crew displayed themselves in bikinis and shorts and busily
took photographs. The sort of day, indeed, that makes cruising
worth while. And then when we finally reached Tarbert, that
wonderfully sheltered harbour, we were absolutely delighted, for
it is a charming centre, with a beautiful setting – indeed we liked
it so much that we stayed on there an extra day in order to help
Martin celebrate his twenty-first birthday.

After Tarbert, the Crinan Canal. This is a much smaller and
narrower canal than the Caledonian, but I had made sure that our
dimensions would just fit in with its maximum requirements of
88 ft. long, 22 ft. beam and 9 ft. 6 in. draft. All the same its winding and torturous passage from Ardrishaig Basin, in the south, to
Crinan at the north end, provided me, as helmsman, with many
headaches. Sometimes, indeed, we could have reached out and
touched the foliage growing on either bank – what we would
have done if we met another large boat like ourselves, goodness
only knows (I discovered later that the lock-keepers pass on information of every craft coming and going, so that if necessary one
can be held back for the arrival of another). Although only nine
miles long the canal was divided by fifteen locks, mostly the old-
fashioned sort where our crew had to lend a hand in winding and
unwinding the gates – but, just as I had imagined, it made a
pleasant change. Sometimes the setting of the canal was quite

breath-taking, winding among huge banks of trees, or opening out upon a picture-book panorama of flat land and distant mountains. In addition to the locks every now and then we came round a bend to encounter a swing bridge, whose operator had to be summoned by an urgent blast on our hooter — sometimes opening his bridge only at the very last moment! Somehow we managed to survive what to me was quite a tricky passage, and ended up in Crinan Basin, along with a dozen or so other craft of various shapes and sizes. Here we had our first exciting view of Hebridean waters, and we felt we were really on our way.

After a call the next day for replenishments at Oban we made our way up Loch Linnhe and Loch Lorne, past the Corran Narrows and Fort William, and came to our second and much larger canal — the Caledonian. Long before we came to the entry port of Corpach we had sensed a formidable change in our surroundings. We were now among *real* mountains — to one side at the rear the towering peaks of Mull, then the equally striking peaks of Morvern — and now at last, stretching away into the very heavens, the huge mountains behind Fort William, rising in the end to Ben Nevis, highest in the British Isles. From the flat sea-lock at Corpach it made a truly impressive sight; and later that evening, after we had made a rather laborious climb through the "staircase" of eight locks at Banavie, Frank and Kate and Jess and I strolled along the quiet leafy banks of the canal and marvelled at the lovely setting.

In fact, as we progressed farther and farther along the sixty-mile long canal (which links the North Sea and the Atlantic Ocean, and provides a safe sheltered passage, as against the rough outer route *via* Cape Wrath and the Minch) we were all agreed that the Caledonian truly justified all the glowing remarks we had heard about its beauty and peacefulness. Possibly what contributed to this was the fact that at three points the canal opens out into a lovely "inland sea" — Loch Lochy, Loch Oichy and Loch Ness: on the other hand I have clear memories of winding canal banks, man-made, often hewn out of rocky countryside, which could rival nature in their beauty.

We had soon reached the highest point at Laggan Locks, and then gradually began descending, notably at Fort Augustus, where there was another "staircase", this time of five descending locks. Here we made our long-awaited entry into the famous Loch Ness, which is itself about 25 miles long. We had the rather uncanny experience of travelling up the loch on an eerie misty afternoon, so that at any moment we were expecting to see "the monster". However, the next day the mist was gone, and it was so sunny and warm that Frank fulfilled his ambition to have a swim in the Ness — the rest of us lacked his courage, and went instead for a long country walk. We had anchored the boat by Temple Pier, opposite Urquhart Castle, and this was the farthest point of our journey east. Here, Frank and Martin had to take their leave, catching a taxi into Inverness to meet the night train bound for London and work. After waving them goodbye we pulled up our anchor and set off back to Fort Augustus, and then on the next day to Banavie and, the following morning, out of the canal altogether.

During this, our first fortnight of the cruise, we had been blessed with excellent weather, every day sunny and blue — so much so that I was constantly taunting Jess, who had dolefully repeated the prognostications of her sister, Marjorie, that it was always raining in Scotland. Now the weather showed signs of flagging, but we did not particularly notice it at the time for we had a new interest — finding Llewellyn. Llewellyn was Kate Baker's son, who had recently married and taken a share in a fishing boat in Scotland, and was reputed to be travelling in it to Mull. Even in the canal we had often strained our eyes trying to identify Llew's craft, which Kate rather vaguely defined as "about twenty-five feet, a converted lifeboat, with a wheel-house". Now, as we proceeded back down Lochs Linnhe and Lorne we kept a hopeful eye out, but with no luck. Towards the end of that day it began raining in that earnest, continual way which we came regretfully to associate

F*

with Scotland, and we were very glad to reach our haven for the night, Loch Aline. The entry was a tricky one over a sand bar, but once inside there was plenty of room to anchor. Indeed, in the starboard corner there were already three or four yachts, and I dutifully brought *Sanu* up alongside them, and we put over the anchor while I reversed . . . or rather, tried to reverse. Suddenly there was an almighty clattering noise, and I hastily put the engine into neutral, while like a bullet Stephen shot below. When he came back, his face was grim.

"It's the coupling — it's slipped again."

This was bad enough news — in addition, already, we could see that our anchor was not holding firm, and we were dragging, and gradually drifting across the loch. There was nothing for it but to pull up the anchor and, now using only our small wing engine, bring the boat round and try anchoring again. This we did; twenty minutes later we were dragging again. Finally, on the third attempt, the anchor seemed to hold, and, exhausted, we went down to supper — aware only too well that the larger problem of the shaft awaited our attention.

That night Stephen, Nicky and Alan spent several hours laboriously fitting the coupling back into place . . . only to find to their chagrin that as soon as we tested the reverse in the morning it slipped out again. There was nothing for it but to try to get the boat out of what suddenly seemed a lonely and god-forsaken loch to somewhere comparatively civilised, where mechanical assistance could be found. Since we could not use the main engine this meant trusting entirely to the small wing engine. If we had been faced with the open sea I would have had my doubts, but since it was only ten miles up the Sound of Mull to Tobermory, the main town of the island, I felt we ought to be able to manage. In fact, our progress was excruciatingly slow, hardly three knots compared to our usual eight — but after three worried hours we finally brought the boat into Tobermory's sheltered harbour and anchored opposite the pier. At once I had the dinghy over the side and rushed ashore to try to find an engineer. The only possible man was busy the rest of that day but he promised to come out at nine o'clock the next morning, and we had to be satisfied with that.

Meantime, seeing posters about advertising the annual cattle show at Salen, farther up the coast, we all piled into one of the MacBrayne's coaches and made a very hazardous and torturous journey whizzing up and down narrow cliff roads. It was interesting to see gathered into one large field what was obviously a very thorough cross-section of the population of Mull (which in all I believe is under 3,000); even more fascinating to see a fine selection of Highland cattle, with their strange "beatnik" hair style. We thoroughly enjoyed the day out and returned full of confidence that in the morning things would soon be put right, and we would be on our way.

In fact, we had an excellent young engineer to attend to the shaft, and he made a fine job of fixing it, so that we were able to start off on the next leg of our journey towards Skye. Unfortunately, had we but known it, our troubles – notably our anchoring troubles, which henceforth were to dominate our Scottish voyaging – were only just beginning. When we took up anchor and set off from Tobermory the weather seemed very sheltered, but no sooner had we shown our nose outside than conditions changed markedly. Usually I always get a weather forecast before moving, but this was midday, and I thought, well, anyway, we can hear the two o'clock forecast. By the time we heard the two o'clock forecast, with its alarming sudden warning of Force 8, possibly gale, for the Hebrides, we had almost reached Ardnamurchan Point . . . where, faced not only by an ugly and rising sea but the added hazard of a real Scottish mist, for the first time in my life I turned my boat back. After all, we were on holiday, boating for pleasure, and none of us fancied three or four hours in a Hebridean gale.

I can hardly doubt that this was a correct decision (in fact the gale conditions persisted for the next three days and brought other ships scuttling into Tobermory) and yet when I think of the con-

sequences. . . . First, we came back into Tobermory and dropped
our anchor rather nearer into shore. An hour or two later, looking
round uneasily, I wondered if we were not dragging a little, but
decided to leave it for the time being. After another hour it became pretty evident . . . around eight o'clock in the evening I
could put off the evil moment no longer, for we were perilously
near the harbour shore.

"Stephen! Alan! Nicky! Afraid we'll have to get the anchor
up, we're dragging badly."

Owing to the fact that the teeth on our winch are rather badly
worn, winding up the anchor chain on *Sanu* is quite a performance, as one person has to stand on the incoming chain in order to
obtain a real grip. However, we duly wound in the anchor and I
put the engine into gear and headed *Sanu* away from the shore.
now a nightmarish experience began. In the first place, because of
the gale quite a lot of boats had accumulated in Tobermory harbour – as I now looked about me they seemed to be dotted about
everywhere. Suddenly I began to realise that finding a safe anchorage was not going to be too easy, with such a large boat as ours.
One of the difficulties at Tobermory is that the harbour is exceptionally deep, right up to the shore, so that one has to anchor
fairly close in. Now, as time after time I took *Sanu* out into the
centre and then headed cautiously close in, I found it impossible to
find a space large enough to enable us to safely drop anchor and
be sure of not swinging back on to one of the dozens of anchored
boats.

At first it seemed fairly amusing, but as time went on and dusk
began to threaten our smiles faded. Once, in desperation, we went
right over to the heavily-wooded far shore and dropped our anchor
in a spot perilously close to the rocky beach. It required only about
quarter of an hour's wait to decide hurriedly that this was no place
to be, and once again we had wearily to pull up the chain. By now
it really was dusk, and suddenly things became very un-funny, and
quite worrying. For here I was at the wheel of what in a fairly

confined space was something of a dangerous monster. A boat like *Sanu*, 60 ft. long and 18 ft. beam, is not exactly easy to manoeuvre at the best of times. Now, as I weaved endlessly between rows of anchored yachts, each time I was forced to slow down, naturally the steerage became more difficult. Added to that the canopy of dusk shrouding the scene meant that everything was twice as difficult. No wonder that one scared yachtswoman, leaning out of her 20-footer, screamed: "Careful, you'll kill us all!"

In fact we didn't really go dangerously close to anyone, but for the helmsman it was a terrible tension; while always there was the haunting knowledge that even if we dropped anchor, we might well drag again (last time when the anchor came up it was covered entirely by thick wads of bright green seaweed, no doubt the cause of its not gripping). In the end, by now quite emotionally exhausted, I felt we could not face the prospect of being at the mercy of our wayward anchor in total darkness. There was one possible alternative. Although we knew we could not go along the steamer quay at Tobermory (in fact because of the gale it was already occupied by a sheltering cruise steamer), there was a smaller stone quay used by local boats, which dried out. This was occupied by one of the Clyde "puffer" boats, small cargo boats that deliver to the islands – but at least the tide was in. Perhaps we could manage to get in and tie up alongside?

And so, shrouded in darkness but guided by the lights of the quay I brought *Sanu* carefully up alongside the SS. *Halycon* . . . and thankfully we tied our ropes to her solid iron samson-post and then hurriedly put down our port leg while we had the chance (when I looked at the echo sounder, we had about one foot of water under us, and the tide was already turning).

"Well," we thought thankfully, "safe at last."

So we were, but there was still a price to pay. Although we put out half a dozen rubber tyres as fenders before going to bed it had not occurred to us that such a large boat – she must have been half as long again as us, and much broader – might actually be considerably shallower than *Sanu*. In fact, whereas we drew seven and a half feet, *Halycon* only drew between five and six feet. As a result, when we were afloat, her wide iron rib, or buffer, was *above* our wooden fender rail — but when we went aground, she continued to drop and drop *and* drop, and eventually her massive fender just broke off a section of ours. It was nothing vitally damaging, but annoying and inconvenient, as well as looking very untidy.

However, during the two enforced gale-bound days we now spent at the quay we soon overcame our annoyance and became friendly with the cheery crew of the *Halycon* — a boat, we learned, that had been playing the islands run for more than fifty years, under the same captain. He was stern, and made in the old-fashioned mould — and every Sunday was to be seen soberly dressed carrying his Bible and heading for the kirk — but he knew every inch of the Hebridean coast, and his young crew had complete faith in him. From what we could make out there was good money in this pleasantly independent form of trading and they were all sad that in another year the boat was due for the scrap yard.

At last the weather improved. Now I was plagued by the fear that during neap tides our boat would never get off the bottom at the quay . . . and in the end, indeed, it was only by arising at 4 a.m. and having the engines running at exactly the moment of high tide that we managed to edge *Sanu* out into deeper water, and be on our way . . . very glad, I must say, to leave Tobermory, picturesque and sheltered though it may be.

This time we were heading round Ardnamurchan and northwards, past Mallaig, and into the Sound of Sleat. *En route* we passed, to port, the formidable mountainous islands of Eigg and Rhum, and the smaller one of Muck. It was a pleasant enough journey (which we could imagine would have been hell in a Force 8 gale) and by midday we had actually reached our fifty-mile-away objective, the renowned and beautiful Loch Duich. I had read so much about this spot, and seen such lovely photographs of its water-surrounded castle, that I was afraid of being disappointed. But in fact it really was most beautiful, especially at the far end of the loch, where the horizon was dominated by mountains known as the Five Sisters. Once again, though, our peace of mind was plagued by anchor trouble; our first anchoring, in what was supposed to be the most sheltered spot, Totaig Bay, lasted five hours, then we began dragging badly. We hauled in, went into the bay again, and this time dropped not only our C.Q.R. anchor on the chain, but also put out our huge old fisherman, on a nylon rope. All to no avail; half an hour ater we were dragging badly towards a small rocky islet. Now when we pulled in the two anchors, the chain and rope became entangled, and we were all swearing and exhausted again when finally I headed *Sanu* away down to the very end of the loch, where we managed to find a really sheltered and peaceful anchorage for the night.

The next morning we were off again, bound at last for the romantic island of Skye itself, the northernmost objective of our trip. Now the weather really had deteriorated, and we were plagued by what we came to recognise as typical Scottish mists, which made navigation more difficult than usual. I was heartily relieved when we reached Raasay Sound, and headed towards Portree, the "capital" of Skye. This was a town and setting not unlike Tobermory, but more highly geared to the tourist industry. However, we were so relieved to be somewhere where we did not have to anchor, being allowed to berth alongside the pier, that we forgave Portree its concessions to tripperdom, and enjoyed two relaxed days exploring the local sights.

By now weather delays had made us very much behind on our itinerary, so at the first reasonable forecast we set off on the last leg of our northern-bound voyage — from Portree up the north-east coast of Skye, and round Eileen Trodday Island, and then down the north-west coast. Scenically it was a magnificent trip, the vast towering cliffs of Skye being quite breath-taking seen from sea-wards . . . but weather conditions altered for the worse after we had rounded Trodday, and for the remaining twenty-five miles, across Vatternish Point and round Dunvegan, we had a big sea coming right across us that was thoroughly uncomfortable.

Loch Dunvegan, I felt sure, would make up for all that. There was a lovely sheltered anchorage just below the famous castle – the only inhabited castle in west Scotland, home of Dame Flora Macleod, and gathering place once a year for Macleods from all over the world. Yes, it was all there, and we came round the last point into sheltered waters and dropped our anchor, and then our other anchor – and, lo and behold, they seemed to be holding, yes, they really were holding. That night, to celebrate this unusual event, we went ashore in the two dinghies, and the older ones among us enjoyed an unexpectedly cheerful evening in the comfortable Dunvegan Hotel. Chugging back in the moonlight was a very romantic experience, and I dismissed from my mind the tiny suspicion that maybe the anchor light on *Sanu* seemed rather farther away than when we had set out.

At least we did have a good night's sleep. But by midday the next day it became only too sadly evident that our old trouble was back, the anchor was dragging – and indeed *Sanu* was getting perilously near to a group of tiny rocky islets that surround the base of Dunvegan Castle.

"Nothing for it," I groaned. "Let's start the engine."

Usually our Kelvin starts on a half swing. Today was going to be different. It would not start on a half swing, nor a whole swing, nor a dozen such swings. Exhausted I stepped aside and Alan took over. Soon the sweat was pouring down his brow, and still the engine would not catch. Becoming uneasy I ran upstairs and took one look. We were indeed very, very close to the rocks. Beside me Stephen looked agitated.

"Start the Lister, Dad – quick!"

I hesitated.

"But that's only a small engine! Will it get us out of here?"

It soon became evident that the question was an academic one:

if the Lister wouldn't get us out, then we would go on the rocks. Quickly we started up our new smaller engine — and for the umpteenth time I thanked my lucky stars that we had put in a second engine. Then we went up deck again and began winding in our two anchors.

Now began what I suppose, in retrospect, was the most excruciating and dangerous experience of the whole trip. For when the anchor finally came up and I put the Lister on to full power and into forward gear, the wind and tide had whipped up so strongly (as seems invariably in our adventures, the weatherman chose this moment to inflict us with what turned out to be the beginning of a real gale, strong even in that supposedly sheltered part) that I just could not bring *Sanu*'s bow round enough to clear the line of the rocky shore ahead of us. I kept going forward until the last possible moment, and then had to hurriedly put her into reverse. But here again, there was a snag — some way behind us lay the rock-infested shore at the base of the castle. Could we manage to come round in reverse enough to clear that and emerge safely, if rearwards, into the fairway? No, it soon became evident, we could not. And so the ridiculous process began, forwards up to one shore, backwards to the opposite shore — without gaining anything, and in fact, very subtly losing some ground so that all the time we were being pushed sideways towards a rocky islet in the centre of the bay.

By now we were all becoming thoroughly alarmed — even, understandably, a little hysterical. To come all these hundreds of miles up to and around the wild Hebrides and then to go aground in a sheltered loch! It was ridiculous. And yet there was no doubt it was going to happen if we did not manage some kind of miracle. We tried everything. At one stage Nicky bravely got into the white motor dinghy with the forlorn idea of tugging the bows round — but by now the waves were so nasty that he was almost swamped and had to swarm back up the rope. After that the three boys stayed down in the engine room trying forlornly to start our recalcitrant main engine.

For myself, I was becoming truly desperate. "Please, *please* come round," I begged *Sanu*'s lumpy bows – but always they half came round and then stuck. It became evident that the forward–reverse procedure could not go on much longer, or we would be thrown on to the middle island. In desperation I considered my one remaining alternative – to go farther in, and try to round the islet from the inside. According to the chart this inner area was strewn with rocks. I had no idea of the depths; it would be an absolute gamble. On the other hand, it would mean turning *Sanu*'s bow to starboard instead of port, and with our wing engine fixed on the port side this would give us a much stronger steerage. Maybe, maybe we could manage? Well, we would have to!

Praying silently, I headed *Sanu* between one rocky shore and the rocky islet, while the rest of my crew who were on deck looked at me in amazement. There wasn't time for any explanations, all we could do was to hold on, while I kept the wheel hard over . . . all the time expecting any moment to hear the horrid crunch of rock driving into *Sanu*'s hull.

It seemed to last an eternity, but I suppose took about three or four minutes – then, miraculously, we had rounded the islet and were safely back in the fairway, heading away from danger, and towards a distant wharf, used by cargo boats, but which now, at all costs, was going to be our home. A few minutes later we were safely tied up there, and trying to unwind our tensed limbs from what was our narrowest ever squeak.

After such an experience we might surely have felt entitled to some relaxation, but the sea is not like that. The wind, which had been freshening, quickly assumed gale proportions, so that even inside the loch we were considerably exposed. The pier at which we were moored was a wooden one, and not over-strong, and now it creaked and groaned. More worryingly, it was the night of an exceptionally high tide, and soon we found to our alarm that *Sanu* appeared to be rising so high that she would surely be on the pier itself. This fate was averted, but our fenders were rendered pretty useless, and the wooden piles of the pier rubbed uncomfortably against our side all night.

On the other hand the sudden gale brought us some good fortune—late that evening a fishing boat came alongside, its crew looking bleary eyed from crossing the Minch in what they swore was a Force 9. Their boat was bound for Mallaig with a big catch of lobsters, so if they put in for shelter, it must have been bad. They were just as friendly as the Belfast men had been, made us take some lobsters as a gift—and later in the evening, on learning of our mechanical trouble, their engineer came across and spent an hour taking ours to pieces and tracing the fault. By then Jess and I had crept miserably to bed, leaving Stephen and Alan to cope, but as the engine-room is beneath our cabin we heard snatches of conversation, and gathered hopefully that some repair was being executed. Sure enough, after a fair while, there was the sudden healthy throb of the Kelvin roaring into life again.

Just as at the beginning of our trip the weather had been kind to us, now it was perverse and tormenting. After a slightly better forecast we set out on the long trip down to Mull, only to encounter perhaps our roughest sea of the trip around the point of Dunvegan—by then we were somewhat committed and grimly ploughed our way through what must have been Force 6–7 until the welcome sight of the small island of Canna offered us a chance to take shelter. Originally Canna had been on our list, then in the effort to make up lost time I had cut it out—now, as we nosed up to the tiny quay in complete shelter from the elements raging outside, I was heartily glad of our choice. Of all the places we visited, in many ways Canna was most intriguing: a small narrow island on which some twenty people live, mostly in crofts, and mostly working for one man, the laird. Despite the tiny population, it was competitively served by two churches—a Roman Catholic one at one end, and a tiny Presbyterian one on the opposite hill. There was no shop, only a small post office—if you wanted provisions you ordered them from Mallaig on the four-times-a-week steamer — and paid about 2s. in the £1 carriage. We talked to one or two inhabitants and found them quite content — and indeed why not, in this age of strain and rush? Everything on Canna seemed pleasantly uncomplicated, and orderly — crops to be got in, animals to be tended, vegetables to be grown in the back garden. The island itself had a strange quiet beauty — and for a more grand landscape there was always the vast tips of Rhum just across the water. We liked Canna very much, and were sorry to leave.

Our next journey took us down past Coll and then round the strange flat-topped Treshnish Isles, and Staffa with its weird Fingal's Cave — and into Loch Lathaich, on the Ross of Mull. According to the Clyde Sailing Club's Guide Book this offered the perfect sheltered anchorage, but for once in a way they must have erred a little, for we found it dreadfully exposed to the prevailing conditions. And once again — I don't want to become a bore but it happened! — we were in serious trouble over anchoring. First the anchor refused to hold at all, though we put out five times the length of chain — so we wound it up again and had another try, this time putting out the old fisherman as well. This time we seemed to be well and truly held, in the lee of a small island, so Alan and Nick and Kate hurriedly got into a dinghy and rowed ashore to a small pier, to go into Bunessan for some provisions. I felt uneasy at thus being left with only Stephen and Jess to help if anything went wrong. Sure enough, after twenty minutes we began dragging badly. And of course when we tried to bring in the anchors they once again got entangled. By this time I had both engines going and was in ample control of the boat, but we simply weren't in a position to do anything about dropping anchors until we had got them unentangled, and on our own couldn't cope.

At this moment Kate and Nick and Alan were to be seen on the pier, getting into the dingy, and we waited . . . and waited until at last it dawned on us that although they were trying desperately to row out, the pressure of wind and waves coming straight on to the shore made it impossible. In fact, they were helpless, tied to the shore! Well, this offered a clue to our own destination: fortunately it was near high tide, and from the chart I estimated that it was just about safe to go alongside the pier. Originally the idea was to pick up the others, but once we were there and found we did float at high tide, we jumped for joy – and put out our leg, and furiously tied up. Safe again from the hazards of anchoring.

After a fascinating visit to Iona, nearby, whose picturesque setting reminded us very much of Cornwall, we were off again on the longest day voyage of the trip, some ninety-five miles past Colonsay and Oronsay and through the Sound of Islay and down the long Mull of Kintyre. We had all heard forbidding tales of this dreaded point, but on this particular day the sea was smooth and unruffled, and we had our second sunniest day of the whole voyage – a glorious trip, right round and into the sheltered loch of Campbeltown. There we were back among fishing boats again, and quite a busy little town, and we able to celebrate our second birthday, this time Demelza's fourteenth, with a dinner at the Royal Hotel. The next morning we were up early and off to Peel on yet another long leg.

At last we felt definitely on the way home, and were glad enough, after our hectic and varied five weeks. There was a momentary and rather ludicrous hold-up when, as we left Peel, our rudder jammed, and we had to manoeuvre ourselves cumbersomely back to the quay in order to fix it – then we were off on another sunny voyage down to Holyhead. Here we were dropping off Kate and Josephine, so instead of anchoring I decided to take *Sanu* into the commercial part of the port, where there is one public quay which the harbour master had told me was available "first come, first served". We found a berth all right, but were immediately assailed by a bevy of officials who warned us of the dire consequences likely to result – our ropes would be parted by the vast wash from the mail steamers, not to mention eight cargo boats coming by in the middle of the night. We were somewhat alarmed and put out extra ropes, but in fact it was all poppycock and we were hardly disturbed at all. And we were very glad we had gone to that quay, for it was near to the railway station where, soon after midnight, we all gave a lively send off to Kate and Josephine on their journey through the night to Cardiff.

Our reason for dropping them off at Holyhead instead of Fishguard was that I had decided to make the trip from Holyhead to St. Ives in one hop. This meant leaving Holyhead in darkness at the unholy hour of 4 a.m. – in order, according to my thrice-checked calculations, to reach St. Ives the next morning about 6 a.m., and so catch the early morning tide and not have to anchor for hours outside. Well, we managed our getaway, and soon the winking light of South Stack was behind us, and we had a trouble-free run down past Bardsey Island and nearly to the Smalls – then our luck changed. Waves got bigger and bigger, the wind blew harder, and the remaining ninety miles, through a long, long night, were about as uncomfortable as had been our very first trip outward. Only by now we were such acclimatized sailors that fortunately no one was sick. We took it in shifts to steer, three hours on and six hours off. My turn was the last one, from three in the morning, and soon after coming on I was delighted to see the beam of Pendeen lighthouse ahead. My pleasure faded somewhat as (a) we failed to find Godrevy light and (b) a thick sleeting rain began blowing in our faces, and clouding the visibility. As a result, until dawn, we were forced to slow down, and content ourselves with two or three nervous trips up and down the coast by Pendeen. At last, however, there was a glimmer of light and soon we identified Zenner Head, and were able to head back to Clodgy Point and the Island. At a few minutes past six o'clock we came zooming into the bay, both engines going full blast in case we missed the tide, and soon after we had nosed up to the quay at St. Ives and were tying up – home at last after a trip which, we calculated, had covered more than 1,500 miles. We were all exhausted and in need of a bath, but we also felt a real pride in the achievement. The next day we took *Sanu* over to Hayle and berthed her safely for the winter. And the day after that – we began thinking about our next season!

12

A Quiet Week-end on the Scillies

AFTER two seasons of savouring the delights of life aboard *Sanu* we approached our third one full of ambitious plans. The Paris venture had whetted our nautical appetites for foreign travel. Why not venture farther still? What about Holland – the Dutch canals? Or even Denmark and Sweden? I had always dreamed of travelling through the famous Gota Canal, from Gothenburg to Stockholm – now I wrote off for details. Meanwhile I accumulated charts and spent many hours pouring over them.

Alas, it was to be a very different sort of season. At the beginning of June we decided to fulfil a long standing promise to our friends in St. Ives – namely, that one week-end we would take them off for a cruise. It was to be a no-children cruise; in fact – a quiet week-end on the Scillies. I must admit we got a lot of fun even out of the planning; there were endless problems over who we should take and not take. At one stage it seemed we were faced with the problem of carrying half of St. Ives, if only out of fear of hurting people's feelings. However, in the end, very sensibly, we cut our list down to ten – four other couples, and ourselves. The others were Christianne and Anthony Richards, two very old friends from the days of St. Hilary; Ken and Jane Moss, our partners on the ill-fated community venture, Benny and Stella, of Troika Pottery; and Jack Richards, of the wrought-iron forge at Lelant, and a friend Gill.

Everything went impressively to plan. Most of the couples had complicated baby-minding arrangements to make, others were notoriously poor time-keepers, yet at the appointed time all were there on the quay — plus quite a few others to cheer us on our way. Thank goodness the harbour was comparatively uncrowded, for *Sanu* is a cumbersome boat to manoeuvre in confined spaces. As it was we gave a toot on the horn and made an impressive reverse sweep before touching ahead and steaming purposefully round the harbour and out into a marvellously calm sea.

The journey across, that sunlit June evening, was undoubtedly the calmest and most enjoyable we had ever made. The bright sunshine, which flooded down generously, illuminated some of the most delectable jewels of the West Cornish coast — Zennor Head, Gurnard's Head (behind, the romantic moors, rising steeply) and then Pendeen's white lighthouse perched on the cliffs . . . and then the weird outline of Botallack mines . . . at last Cape Cornwall, and then a gradual receding of the land away to port as we headed out on our course of 245°. Fine day though it was there was a certain amount of heat haze about so that eventually we lost the mainland without having yet sighted the islands. However, we caught a glimpse of the Seven Stones light vessel on our starboard just where it should be, and we continued to peer eagerly ahead. I have always thought that the first appearance of those misty humps of land on the horizon is an unforgettable experience — and sure enough, now, one by one, they began to emerge. My friends, most of whom had never made the trip before, were entranced : especially when, as an added tit-bit, we encountered a school of basking sharks, lazily encircling the ship.

As we drew nearer and began to trace the outlines of Round Island, then St. Martin's with its familiar day-mark, and finally the long line of the largest island, St. Mary's, so the enchantment grew. And why not? — for there ahead of us glowed a reddy-gold ball of fire in the sky — as I brought *Sanu* round Peninnis Head and weaved past the Spanish Ledges and Bartholomew buoy and into St. Mary's Sound, it was very much like cruising into a fairy world. Islands, islands everywhere, glimmering in the bright sunshine — and at last ahead of us the familiar and ever attractive port of St. Mary's, where we tied up smartly and then hurried ashore for a last drink at the "Mermaid" before returning to the boat for our first celebratory supper. At midnight some of the party went for a moonlit trip in our *Zodiac* dinghy while the rest of us relaxed, sun-drenched and happy with our progress.

"Ah, but you haven't seen anything yet," I said grandly. "Just wait until tomorrow — I'll take you over to Tresco and we'll anchor there for the night. That's an experience you won't forget, I can promise."

The next afternoon I took *Sanu* and our friends over to Tresco, waiting until close on high tide before venturing through the torturous channel across Tresco Flats. Fortunately we had made this trip several times before, so we knew the hazards, and also the recognised anchorage just below Cromwell Castle. After one or two alarming experiences of anchor-dragging the previous summer, because of a mixture of seaweed and rock, I had become somewhat obsessive about making sure the anchor was well and truly dug in: and so on this occasion I decided our first effort left us too near the shore and made my "crew" pull in the chain so that we could move farther out into the middle of the channel and drop again. This time everything went very smoothly, the echo sounder showed thirty feet of water at high tide so we put out ninety feet of chain and then waited while *Sanu* drifted back until the chain took up and it became apparent she was well and truly held. Being naturally suspicious, I kept checking during the next hour or so, and nothing changed: Hangman's Isle was where it should be, Cromwell Castle a respectable distance away. Relieved, I responded to the call that supper was ready, and we gathered in the saloon to enjoy the second of our vast cruising meals.

Afterwards, at about nine-thirty, with the sunset forming all around us in fascinating hues, it seemed a good idea to row ashore for the last hour at the "New Inn", Tresco, that cosy tavern of whose delights we had boasted to our friends. I took a last captainly look round : *Sanu* rode peacefully at her anchor, the land was where it always had been, the tide was ebbing, there was hardly any wind . . . everything was still and peaceful. Why, then, did I have just the faintest of feelings, a strange hint of a disinclination to go ashore? Of course, I told myself sternly, it was all imagination, some relic of experiences in Scotland; mustn't give way to blind impulses — come along now, the *Zodiac* is ready to make its second journey.

I put on the anchor light, made sure everything else was in order, and got aboard the *Zodiac*. As we glided down the channel towards New Grimsby Quay we all looked back at our mother ship, riding proudly in the middle of the channel — suddenly appearing, from our lowly level, even grander and more impressive than perhaps she really was. I remember vividly how I watched the familiar outline, and that single bright light, until we had passed out of sight into New Grimsby.

That evening at the "New Inn", Tresco, had been intended to be the *pièce de résistance* of our trip. We had always liked this friendly little pub, tucked away in the middle of the remote island — far, far from both crowds and officious authority. On a summery afternoon you can sit out in the garden sipping your drink under the bright sunshine . . . and in evenings it is cosy enough in the saloon, and if your attention wanders — well it will soon be riveted by the fantastic collection of photographs adorning (indeed almost covering) the walls. Photographs, not of some pretty scene, or some old-world fisherman, or indeed monster fish — no, photographs of nothing but — wrecks. I should imagine every wreck that has ever taken place around the Scillies is duly documented on those walls. The result, is a macabre sight, indeed. Barques, ketches, schooners, cargo boats, yachts, motorboats — there they all are in various postures of discomfort; if not broken into pieces, then hanging from sharp rocks, or grounded for ever on big banks.

Did someone jokingly make the remark, that evening, "Let's hope we're never up there?" I don't know. But I do remember, curiously, being haunted – indeed possessed is not too strong a word for it – by a strong feeling of unease. Looking back I can see quite clearly now that I did not really want to leave *Sanu* and go ashore, that I had no pleasure about taking my friends into the "New Inn" (whereas I had expected to really enjoy showing them round) – and that I was ill at ease the whole of the hour and a half we were ashore. In short, at least as any believer in the psychic would tell you, I was receiving intimations of impending trouble, and I should have had the sense to respond to them.

But, of course, we close ourselves up with our material certitudes, and so I tried to shrug away this feeling of unease, and to attend to my friends' comfort. I still have a vivid picture of them all sitting in the window of the saloon – all looking curiously sober, for in fact that evening was a surprisingly subdued one. Nobody got drunk or merry, and the most lively time was when a few went into the games room and played Russian bar billiards. I was not one of them; I felt too depressed. At one stage I saw a fisherman from Bryher I had met in the past, and had a few words with him. I was really seeking some reassurance from him that our boat would be perfectly safe anchored where she was; after all it was the official anchorage, marked on all the Admiralty charts. Unfortunately he shook his head and said we would have done better to anchor lower down. This hardly put me at ease, and soon I was just praying for time to be called, so that we could get back to *Sanu*.

When we had walked back to New Grimsby Quay, Jack, Jess and Gill, and Ken and Jane decided to walk back along the cliffs to Cromwell Castle, from where we could pick them up later, while Benny, Stella, Anthony, and Chris and I made the trip back in the *Zodiac*. By now I was more and more anxious to be back. . . . It was all the more frustrating that the tide had gone right out, leaving the *Zodiac* high and dry so that we had to drag it a long way down to the water's edge. Even then it was quite a job to get her afloat, clear of weeds and rocks — matters not being helped by the solid presence of a seven-months pregnant Christianne! At one stage we thought we were clear and began rowing furiously for several moments before realising we were on a sand bank. At last, however, we managed to get clear and steered our way out of the harbour and round the point into the centre of the channel.

"Where's the boat?" said someone.

I shall never, never forget the traumatic moment when I peered ahead through the twilight and saw at once that *Sanu* was not where she should be. What I *expected* to see was the bright anchor light somewhere in the middle of the channel, with the outline of Cromwell Castle well over to starboard. What I actually saw was the firm outline of Cromwell Castle seemingly in the centre, and the anchor light, brightly burning, well over to the right, against a dark, menacing background of cliffs and rocks.

"She's aground!" I cried out in anguish. "She's on the rocks!"

She was, too — high and dry on the rocks, and heeling over at an alarming angle of about 50 degrees, her lower deck still awash with water from a tide which was almost at its lowest, leaving about four feet around the hull.

The next few minutes were chaotic. We got *Zodiac* alongside and two of us clambered aboard. It was an eerie experience trying to claw our way upward over a deck on which, earlier, we had been sunbathing. Somehow we managed to make our way to the engine room stairs, and to go down these. Weirdly enough, the electric lights were still working, and by these we saw that there was a certain amount of water around the engine, but not an overwhelming amount (naturally enough, since it was low tide!).

Since there was obviously nothing we could do for the moment we hastened back to the *Zodiac* and tried to row across to the small sandy beach beyond the rocks. Unfortunately there was so much clinging seaweed that we simply could not get any pull on the oars, so there was nothing for it but to climb out and pull her ashore, waist deep in water. This proved a somewhat alarming experience for we were treading gingerly over sharp and slippery rocks – once my foot went down in a crevice and I visualised a quickly broken leg – but somehow we managed to reach the shore, where by now the walkers had arrived.

Not bothering to explain – and after all the eerie moonlit scene was explanation enough – I left the others and began a nightmare climb up the cliffs and along the winding path that finally brought me down into New Grimsby. I remembered that the only public telephone box on the island lay some way farther along the lane, and ran most of the way. When at last, breathless, I tugged open the door it was to find facing me, tied firmly across the receiver, a large white card bearing the brusque message, "Out of Order".

Fortunately it was not far back to the "New Inn", and though it was getting late I found the landlord still up and he at once led me to his phone. The operator put me through to the Coastguard Station where the officer took down the relevant facts as I spurted them out, rather disjointedly, then told me to stay where I was while he got in touch with the Lifeboat Station. A few minutes later the phone rang and I found myself speaking to the Lifeboat Station at St. Mary's, from where the decision was taken that as the boat was aground at the moment nothing much could be done until towards high tide, a few hours later.

Soon I found myself clambering down the cliffs on to the little beach again. All the way back, stumbling over half-seen boulders, I kept shaking my head and saying to myself, "This isn't real – it can't be really happening – not to me!" But alas, as soon as I came back to the fateful scene I saw it was all only too vividly real. There was my beloved *Sanu* reeling over like a drunken thing, with the anchor light still bizarrely blazing through the night.

And on the shore were gathered a somewhat bedraggled crew. However, thanks to smart work by my wife and Jack, who swam out to the boat and managed to rescue a couple of sleeping bags and one or two coats hanging in the wheelhouse, still then above water level, there was some sort of protection. We pulled coats and sleeping bags around us and nestled close together on the tiny beach, trying to keep warm. In any other circumstances it might have seemed rather romantic, but as things were. . . . And then, as if to emphasise that this was just not our lucky night, it began to rain. Soon the drizzle had become a downpour. At that moment a light appeared along the cliffpath and a local coast-guard arrived to see if he could help. On his suggestion we left our sandy, now very wet beach and climbed over the rocks up into the shelter of Cromwell Castle itself. I doubt if this Ancient Monument has ever housed a more motley collection of forlorn mariners — but anyway, shelter it did provide. The women in the party, and one of the men, stayed there for the rest of the night, fortified by some hot coffee kindly brought by the coast-guard, while the remaining men, after waiting another hour, went back to the dinghy and rowed out to *Sanu*, to wait aboard her sloping side for the arrival of the lifeboat.

By now the water had risen considerably and we found it impossible to do much more than cling to the bulwarks or lean at a steep angle in the wheelhouse. At one stage, in order to re-tie the dinghy, we had to slide down to the lower part of the deck and found ourselves working with water creeping up around our chests, an eerie and unwelcome sensation.

At last we saw the bright beam of the lifeboat searchlight as she made her cautious way down Tresco Channel towards us. After a spot of manoeuvring they landed a yellow oil-skinned crew member to take a quick look at the state of things. His

G

decisive comment was to the point. "She'm as full as an egg!" he
cried out to his skipper.

There was nothing, it appeared, that could possibly be done
now, for the boat was not only heeled over but full of water,
and would never right of her own accord. Something might be
attempted at the next low tide — meantime we had better allow
ourselves to be removed to safety by the lifeboat. Clinging forlornly to our faithful *Zodiac* we got pulled over to the lifeboat
and were soon hauled up and taken down to the main cabin. We
had, of course, explained our companions' plight, and after a lot
of rather officious radio conversations back to headquarters it was
decided that the best thing would be to leave the people asleep
in the Castle till dawn and then for them to join us at New
Grimsby Quay, so that the whole group could be transported to
St. Mary's.

By now I suppose the four of us looking a sorry sight — wet
through, shipless, weary, bleary — at any rate the lifeboat men
did their best to alleviate our misery. Out came the inevitable
self-heating cans of soup, of which I had often read but never
expected to see under such circumstances. It seemed to us rather
amusing that after puncturing several holes in the cans the crew-
man found he hadn't a match to light the heater and had to
borrow a lighter from one of us. But at any rate the soup was
piping hot and very welcome, and so was the cup of tea made
later when the ladies had joined us.

Next, our whole party was taken over to St. Mary's. So far
things had carried the overtones of a dream, or rather a nightmare, but when we now heard the radio operator ringing through
to arrange for a representative of the Shipwrecked Mariners'
Association to meet us, we began to realise how grimly real our
situation was. I think we must all have suffered something of a
relapse on that final journey, because when we landed on the
quay at St. Mary's about six o'clock in the morning, not only did
we look the parts of shipwrecked mariners — we felt them, too!

Here I must interpose a tribute to this body of which we knew so little before, but which I understand has branches not only in every British port but in ports all over the world. Although it was a Sunday morning the local representative of the Association was awaiting us on the quay and had already managed to arrange for a local café to open extra early — by seven o'clock all ten of us were sitting down to a welcome hot breakfast. Nor was this all. While we ate, our new counsellor made a quick list of essential clothing needed, went off – and in half an hour was back bearing the precious bundles. When I add that during the same early period of the morning he also found billets for us for the ensuing night, as well as providing tickets for the journey back to the mainland on the Scillonian, then perhaps I convey some idea of the essentially down-to-earth, practical help given by the Association. An organisation by the way which recognises no differences or barriers – to them a shipwrecked mariner, whether master or mate, crew or passenger, is just that: someone suddenly in serious trouble, most likely shocked and certainly distressed, and needing immediate sustenance.

Although we felt as if we had been up all night (and had!) we were naturally concerned about the fate of *Sanu*, and later that morning several of us gathered on the quay at St. Mary's to accompany a party of men, led by the cox of the lifeboat, who were going to have a shot at raising our boat. So at midday there we were once again opposite that now rather sinister looking Cromwell Castle, leaning over the rails of a local tug and watching the combined efforts of two divers, three fire-brigade men and several others. The idea was to tie a series of large empty oil drums to the fallen side of *Sanu* and, with the pumps going full blast at the same time, to encourage her to come level with the rising tide. Alas, despite several hours of hard work, the attempt failed – hardly surprisingly, as the divers had already found several holes in the bottom, caused by the weight of the boat resting on sharp rocks.

The next day a more ambitious attempt was made, this time under the direction of the Isles of Scilly Steamship Company, who mustered a large contingent of men, plus this time a long dumb barge, used for carrying local freight. Oil drums were again used, but this time put inside the boat, at a low level in the bilges. The barge was attached to the low fallen side of *Sanu*, while at the same time lines were run by block and tackle from the anchor winch and, at the rear, the mast, over to some rocks below the Castle. At low tide the pumps began working furiously in an effort to reduce the amount of water inside the boat.

During all these operations our spirits had flagged considerably and we had begun to resign ourselves to the eventual loss of *Sanu*. It was obvious indeed that if she stayed much longer where she was, poised on an evil looking range of rocks — and especially if there was a change of weather — she would soon get damaged beyond all hope of repair. We had already, the previous day, had to watch the inexorable tide rise up and cover not merely her decks but the sides and finally the roof of our deckhouse cabin, and most of the wheel-house, so that all to be seen sticking forlornly out of the water were the two masts. We felt we could not bear to go through all this again, to no avail.

Fortunately, things turned out more happily. Under the combined pressure of all the forces aiming at the same result *Sanu* slowly, with the incoming tide, began to correct her list and finally came almost level — propped on the other side by a leg we had put out. She was still, alas, pretty full of water, so that she presented a very odd appearance, being awash — but at least she was upright. Now at last the two divers could really get underneath and attach temporary plywood patches to the holes. It was decided we had missed the chance of getting her off on this high tide and the best thing was to wait for the next low tide, then pump out at full pressure with a view to finally pulling her off as the tide came in again.

It was a long and cold night watch, but one that filled with tension as the first light of dawn began to glimmer over the distant humps — for high tide was approaching. Now there was a final burst of activity: ropes were rearranged, pumps blasted away, and now the tow wire had been attached to the waiting tug boat. Probably it had been imagined that the tow off would take some time — but, wonder of wonders, as soon as the tide was high enough, *Sanu* eased off her uncomfortable perch at the first gentle pull. Hey presto — she was afloat again!

I suppose it is ridiculous to be too sentimental about that moment which after all was only part of a long slog — but somehow it was *the* other traumatic moment, to balance that awful first one — the wonderful, dawn-kissed moment when suddenly I saw a sight I had begun to think I would never see again — that proud, curving bow, elaborately decorated by my artist son-in-law with the bold lettering S A N U, swishing through the waters again, a boat alive, risen from the dead. I think all the men felt very much the same, hardened though they were — for no seaman can bear to see a boat ravished in this way — and we towed *Sanu* gently through Tresco flats in a mood almost of quiet exhilaration, at last pulling her high up at the quay at St. Mary's, for the pumps to get to work to try to reduce the water level inside.

By now all my companions had gone home, but of course it was essential for me to stay on; the whole business of saving *Sanu* was only just beginning. Getting her up from the sea bed was of course a vitally important operation, but she was still badly wounded and would need many months of treatment. In fact, the next day she had to be taken away from the quay and beached high up in St. Mary's bay, in order to give the shipwrights a chance to put temporary patches on her hull.

It was a depressing sight, now, to see *Sanu* up on the beach, with her legs out, exposed in all her wounded nakedness. In point of fact there were four holes on her port side, one or two gashes on the keel, and a hole on the starboard side. The holes were not very large ones, really, and in themselves did not represent major damage. No, the major damage became only too evident when I climbed aboard and stood in the wheel-house and looked down at the diesel-stained sea-drenched pandemonium below. In their efforts to save the boat by plugging her with empty oil drums, the shipwrights had had to rip many parts away from the walls, and even cut up some of the floor. The gas-cooker lay upside down in a corner, the heater was in the bilge, the new Torgem fire was in pieces, water tanks lay strewn around — even the staircase had been dismantled! The engine room was even worse to see, because of course I knew that salt water had a serious effect on such mechanisms. If only the engines could have been stripped there and then, or at least emptied out and filled with detergents, then they might have been saved. Unfortunately the Isles of Scilly Steamship Company, who had worked readily and excellently to raise the boat, could not spare an engineer for this work and by the time we finally got the boat over to the mainland, it was really too late.

Now began the endless permutations of insurance procedure. At least thank goodness I *was* insured – though not, I began to apprehend, for enough. *Sanu* had cost me £4,000, I had spent another £1,000 at least on improving her, so I had insured for for £5,000 – but in fact she was worth a good deal more than that (several people on the Scillies reckoned £10,000 at least). Now as all the bills began to mount up, I began to grow alarmed. The lifeboat, the coast-guards, the skin-divers, the shipwrights, the fitters, the boatmen, the fire service . . . heaven knew what they were all going to cost. Then there was the cost of a surveyor sent from London by the insurance company.

The days passed. After humming-and-hawing the Isles of Scilly Steamship Company said they couldn't possibly tackle the repair job, so we immediately tried Holman and Sons, a big firm at Penzance who have their own dry dock. We didn't expect to get anywhere, but of course we had forgotten it was in the middle of the seaman's strike, so that Holman's were without work. In no time at all one of their representatives had flown over on the B.E.A. helicopter and made an on-the-spot inspection and they had agreed to do the job. What's more they fixed up with a skipper of a fishing boat on the Scillies to tow *Sanu* to Penzance for £80.

Cheered by this sign of progress – heartened by an assurance by the secretary of the Isles of Scilly Steamship Company that his bill for their work in rescuing *Sanu* would be a very reasonable one, simply the cost of labour — I went home (ignominiously) on the tripper steamer, *Queen of the Isles*. Of course, the moment I stepped off the gangway at St. Ives there were all the familiar faces of local fishermen — many of them, to do them credit, genuinely sympathetic, but quite a few only too obviously not sorry to see our balloon burst. I felt like slinking away quietly, but of course one just had to get through all the inevitable questions and pointed remarks.

I was glad to be home, but relief was short-lived. The next day Holman's calmly announced that they couldn't do the job after all. The insurance assessor, like me, was furious, but there was nothing we could do about it but get in touch with the only other local firm likely to be able to tackle the job, the Falmouth Boat Company, with whom *Sanu* had been berthed in her first season. Once again a man came over to inspect, once again our assessor made a visit — once again the job was accepted. This time, fortunately, the firm stuck to their agreement, and the next day a Falmouth tug arrived and towed the still patched-up *Sanu* (still taking in a little water) over to Falmouth and the Flushing boatyard of the Falmouth Boat Company.

There began the long, long process of resurrection. First *Sanu*'s massive frame had to be winched slowly out of the water and up runners into a large hangar — so big was she that she only just got under the roof, and that after removing the masts. When a few days later Jess and I went over to take a look, it was a disheartening sight. The workmen had just finished removing the temporary patches, so that *Sanu* was exposed, as it were with her raw wounds, several gaping holes through which you could look straight up into the saloon. Up there, of course, there was utter chaos; altogether the boat seemed in a sorry state. However, it could be put right, we knew that — it was just a question of time.

Time, indeed, seemed to pass endlessly as we waited anxiously for news of progress. Repairing a boat of *Sanu*'s size, of course, is no light task, but often we felt things really should be getting along a little quicker. However, gradually, as week followed week, things began to take shape. The old planks were taken out, new ones cut and put in and bolted down: the Kelvin engine was saved, but the Lister side-engine was found to be ruined, which meant ordering another one. Then there was the whole electrical system to be renewed — the complete water system, involving eight separate tanks and piping, to be cleaned out — the Calor gas stove and heater replaced — the bedding, mattresses, seats — goodness, it seemed there was no end to it all. And the cost! By now the bills had come in from the Isles of Scilly Steam-ship Company, very much higher than I had been expecting. When the bills from Falmouth also began mounting we realised that there was every likelihood of the cost outweighing the whole of our insurance.

As it happened, long before the accident, we had arranged to let our house at St. Ives for the whole of August in anticipation of a cruising holiday in *Sanu*. This arrangement naturally still held, and so, as the boat was still not ready, we were temporarily homeless. At the back of our minds we still clung to the hope that maybe *Sanu* would be repaired in time for a last cruise, so we decided now the sensible thing would be to rent somewhere over at Falmouth, and start doing as much work as we could on the boat ourselves — thus saving both time and money.

And that was how we spent the whole of the hot, calm August. We were lucky enough to rent a small house at Greenbank, Falmouth, which looks out over that marvellous harbour, and from here every morning Martin, Stephen and his friend Nicky, would motor across in the *Zodiac* to the Little Falmouth Boat-yard at Flushing and go to work, alongside the other more pro-fessional boatyard workers. The boys enjoyed the experience hugely, and I must say got through a formidable amount of work, including two paintings of the exterior and hull and a lot of useful interior decoration. Meantime Jess and I invariably had to pop down to the chandlers in Falmouth to obtain more materials before driving over to swell the labouring staff.

Every time we arrived at the boatyard we secretly hoped for some miracle. Mr Hodges, the works manager, had a persuasively optimistic sort of outlook, so that often we felt that everything was on the point of being finished, but somehow there were always hold-ups. Meantime, our friends Frank and Kate Baker had arrived in the district, hopeful like ourselves of participating in one last cruise. As day after day, week after week went by, we all began to lose hope.

And then one marvellous day Mr Hodges mentioned casually that *Sanu* was going to be winched back into the water, and tied up at the quay for the last jobs to be done there. We could hardly believe it all, but sure enough the huge massive frame — now glistening in bright new paint — edged slowly down into the water, with Jess taking a ciné film of the memorable occasion. It wasn't, of course, quite the end of the matter : there were infuriating last-minute hitches, such as the non-appearance of a vital regulator, but at last there came the day of the sea trials — and once more I was at *Sanu*'s helm, Mr Hodges beside me, threading a rather anxious way between the racing yachts of local sailing clubs. We spent an hour or so travelling across to the Carrick Roads and back, and then tied up at a buoy off the Prince of Wales Pier, relatively satisfied with the boat and main engine but worried about the new side-engine, where oil pressure was alarmingly low. That same night Mike Peters came over from St. Ives and quickly remedied this fault, so we were all at once in a position where — though without the regulator so that we could only charge our batteries on the main engine — we still had time for a "last fling" cruise across to Brittany.

Needless to say, after a month of dead calm weather, everything changed, winds were Force 6 and 7, and we had to stay at our buoy another three days. At long last, about eight o'clock one evening on the very last day of August, we slipped our mooring, and headed out from Falmouth. The weather was still very unsettled, but the forecasts offered hopes of a temporary reprieve, and we crossed our fingers. I must say we all felt strangely uplifted as once more *Sanu*'s stout bows were pointed seawards . . . and in the gathering dusk we left the winking light of St. Anthony's Head lighthouse behind us and headed up past the Lizard coast, on a course for Ushant, 100 miles away.

It was, alas, a hard night's work! Going across the Channel meant we had to take the waves on our beam and the going was consistently uncomfortable, so that one by one we succumbed to the miseries of being sea-sick. However, that was to be the lesser of our worries. A more pressing one began to haunt me about eight o'clock the next morning, when I became increasingly anxious to see the outline of Ushant, a familiar landmark to shipping from many parts of the world. I had read that it was a very flat island, but it had not really occurred to me that I might have difficulty in sighting it—now I regretted bitterly I had not planned our journey so that we reached the area in darkness, when we would have sighted one or more of Ushant's five lights, at least one of them visible for twenty miles.

After another hour, and then yet another, and with our log registering at least 110 miles, I began really to worry. I had mapped a complete course from Falmouth *via* Ushant and the Chausse de Sein down to Audierne, a fishing port on the west coast of Brittany . . . but this all presupposed we sighted Ushant, and from there followed a new course to the Ile de Sein buoy. Now, all at once, I had the alarming sensation of feeling completely lost. Wherever I looked, no matter how much I strained my eyes, I could see nothing—no land, no Ushant—not even a ship.

I suppose the long night at sea had exhausted me so that my nerves were on edge. At the same time, I was conscious suddenly of being responsible for a dozen other human beings, including a year-old baby and, from my careful studying of the navigation charts I knew that the coast of Brittany was a most inhospitable one if you had no idea where you were.

For this reason when someone mooted the idea of turning to port and heading for the coast of France — which must be there somewhere! — I felt decidedly unenthusiastic.

"You've no idea what you're saying — why, it's *littered* with rocks and reefs — we might arrive in the middle of a shoal or something. No, it's far too dangerous." I paused and then, clinging to the one salient factor of identification, I declared, though rather weakly, "There's only one thing I dare do, that's turn round and follow the opposite course back to Falmouth."

It shows how mentally exhausted I was even to contemplate such a drastic course, for the strain of yet another twelve-hour trip would have been quite unbearable. Fortunately, the others talked me round, sufficiently at least to agree to have a shot at striking somewhere on the French coast, and somewhat uneasily I brought *Sanu*'s bow round and headed eastwards.

Just then we sighted a ship — no, indeed, *two* ships — over on our port. After a hasty discussion we decided that being completely lost we really ought to explore every means of finding out where we were — and so it would be a good idea to send up a flare to attract attention (we envisaged going alongside and getting our position). It was the first time we had ever had occasion to use a flare, but after reading the instructions carefully, Alan took one out and, when he stood up near the bow, pulled the release lever and sent up a huge cloud of orange smoke, which billowed back in the wind.

Here I should explain that one or two of the boys had been really ill on the voyage and so had not appeared for some time up in the wheelhouse. At this particular moment a rather weak Martin chose to stagger up the aft cabin stairs. He had just woken up from a heavy sleep, after being ill, and noticed to his alarm that the bilges appeared rather full. Seeking to pass on this knowledge he hurried on to the deck — just in time to get a sharp crack on the head from the mizzen boom. Staggering slightly from the blow he was then horrified to be enveloped in great clouds of orange smoke. This was too much for the dazed Martin. Not only was the boat in danger of sinking, it was also burning!

"Fire!" cried Martin at the top of his voice. "Fire — Fire — Fire!"

This cry was taken up, behind him, by Nicky, and the two of them came running up to the front of the boat — there, somewhat sheepishly, to discover Alan frantically trying to light a second flare. When it finally went up the wind had changed and now blew all the filthy sulphur fumes directly back into the wheel-house, which didn't help matters. What upset us most, however, was that despite the two flares, despite the fact we flew a flag signalling we required assistance, neither of the two ships paid the slightest attention — and being larger and faster than us, had soon passed by on their way.

After this, our faith in fellow humanity sadly shattered, we felt bound to give ourselves up to the whims of Fate — which, fortunately, now leaned in our favour. After keeping on our eastward course for a few more miles the sharp eyes of Gill suddenly spotted a very distant buoy. I was unimpressed. "It could be anywhere — there are dozens of buoys along the coast — dozens!"

Nevertheless, out of all those buoys, by a blessed miracle this one turned out to be the very one that marked the outer shoals of the *Chausse de Sein* — or "The Saints", as they are popularly known. We had, in fact, turned into the coast almost at exactly the right place, and were now dead on course for the distant point, and beyond that — Audierne.

The relief was incredible. In the back of my mind I had imagined a hopeless quest, and then darkness falling, our boat still at sea, the unknown sea . . . no, it had not borne thinking about. And now all at once everything changed, even the weather. A bright afternoon sun shone down on us — and here ahead were the bright white houses of the Ile de Sein, our first sight of the Brittany coast. . . . Two hours later we were heading in past Raoulic jetty through the narrow channel that led into the centre of Audierne itself — and tying up almost opposite the very restaurant where, later that evening, we all celebrated the beginning of yet another exciting adventure of going "to sea with *Sanu*".